Illustrator:
Howard Chaney

Editor:
Marsha Kearns

Editorial Project Manager:
Ina Massler Levin, M.A.

Editor in Chief:
Sharon Coan, M.S. Ed.

Art Director:
Elayne Roberts

Associate Designer:
Denise Bauer

Cover Artist:
Sue Fullam

Product Manager:
Phil Garcia

Imaging:
David Bennett
Alfred Lau

Consultant:
Sandra Lowry
Executive Director
Indian Education Center
Susanville, CA

Publishers:
Rachelle Cracchiolo, M.S. Ed.
Mary Dupuy Smith, M.S. Ed.

Learning Through Literature
NATIVE AMERICANS
INTERMEDIATE

Authors:
Liz Rothlein, Ed. D.
and Sharon Vaughn, Ph. D.

Teacher Created Materials, Inc.
P.O. Box 1040
Huntington Beach, CA 92647
©*1996 Teacher Created Materials, Inc.*
Made in U.S.A.
ISBN-1-55734-476-0

The classroom teacher may reproduce copies of materials in this book for classroom use only. The reproduction of any part for an entire school or school system is strictly prohibited. No part of this publication may be transmitted, stored, or recorded in any form without written permission from the publisher.

Table of Contents

Introduction 4

Plains

Black Elk, A Man with a Vision 5
(Available in USA, Childrens Press; Canada, Riverwood Publishers; AUS, Franklin Watts)

Sitting Bull 10
(Available in USA, Simon & Schuster; Canada, Distican; UK, Simon & Schuster; AUS, Prentice Hall)

Sky Dogs 15
(Available in USA, Harcourt Brace Jovanovich; Canada & UK, HBJ; AUS, HBJ AUS)

Cherokee Summer 20
(Available in USA, Holiday House; Canada, Thomas Allen & Son; UK & AUS, Baker & Taylor Int.)

Where the Buffaloes Begin 25
(Available in USA, Viking Childrens Books; Canada, Penguin Books Canada; UK, Penguin UK; AUS, Penguin Books AUS)

Her Seven Brothers 29
(Available in USA, Bradbury Press; Canada, Doubleday Dell Seal; UK, Bantam Doubleday Dell; AUS, Transworld Publishers)

First Came the Indians 34
(Available in USA, Antheneum; Canada, Distican; UK, Simon & Schuster; AUS, Prentice Hall)

Buffalo Woman 39
(Available in USA, Bradbury Press; Canada, Doubleday Dell Seal; UK, Bantam Doubleday Dell; AUS, Transworld Publishers)

Iktomi and the Buffalo Skull 44
(Available in USA, Orchard Books; Canada, Gage Distributors; UK, Baker & Taylor Int.; AUS, Franklin Watts AUS)

The Cheyenne 49
(Available in USA, Childrens Press; Canada, Riverwood; AUS, Franklin Watts)

Southwest

The Storyteller 54
(Available in USA, Rizzoli Int.; Canada, McClelland & Stewart; UK, Macmillian General. Bks; AUS, Macmillian Dist. Services)

Aztec, Inca, and Maya 60
(Available in USA, Alfred A. Knopf; Canada, Penguin Books Canada; UK, Dorling Kindersley; AUS, Harper Collins)

Arrow to the Sun 66
(Available in USA, Viking; Canada, Penguin Books Canada; UK, Penguin UK; AUS, Penguin Books AUS)

The Hopi 71
(Available in USA, Childrens Press; Canada, Riverwood; AUS, Franklin Watts)

Hawk, I'm Your Brother 76

Table of Contents (cont.)

Southwest (cont.)

Big Thunder Magic 81
  (Available in USA, Greenwillow; Canada, Gage Distributors; UK, International Book Distributors; AUS, Kirby Book Co.)

Annie and the Old One 86
  (Available in USA, Little, Brown & Co.; Canada, Little, Brown; UK, Little, Brown Ltd.; AUS, Penguin)

The Legend of the Indian Paintbrush 91
  (Available in USA, Putnam; Canada, BeJo Sales; UK & AUS, Warner Int.)

Knots on a Counting Rope 97
  (Available in USA, Henry Holt & Co., Inc.; Canada, Fitz Henry & Whiteside; UK, Pan Demic Ltd.; AUS, CIS Publishers)

Northwest

Brother Eagle, Sister Sky 102
  (Available in USA, Scholastic, Inc.; Canada, Scholastic; UK, Scholastic Party Ltd.; AUS, Ashton Scholastic Party Ltd.)

North and Southeast

Little Firefly: An Algonquian Legend 108
  (Available in USA, Watermill Press; Canada, Penguin Books Canada; UK, Penguin UK; AUS, Penguin Books AUS)

Pocahontas, Daughter of a Chief 113
  (Available in USA, Childrens Press; Canada, Riverwood Publishers; AUS, Franklin Watts)

The Seminole 117
  (Available in USA, Childrens Press; Canada, Riverwood Publishers; AUS, Franklin Watts)

The Chippewa 122
  (Available in USA, Childrens Press; Canada, Riverwood Publishers; AUS, Franklin Watts)

The Mohawk 128
  (Available in USA, Childrens Press; Canada, Riverwood Publishers; AUS, Franklin Watts)

The Woman Who Fell From the Sky 132
  (Available in USA, William Morrow & Co.; Canada, Gage Distributors; UK, International Book Co.; AUS, Kirby Book Co.)

Corn Is Maize: The Gift of the Indians 138
  (Available in USA, Thomas Y. Crowell; Canada & UK; Harper Collins Publishers, Ltd.; AUS, Harper Collins)

Introduction

Learning Through Literature: Native Americans is a 144-page resource book for use in the intermediate elementary classroom. The book is divided into five sections that represent the major geographic divisions of Native American tribes of the Americas: **Plains, Southwest, Northwest,** and **North** and **Southeast.** The title, author, and publisher of each book are provided, along with a brief summary of its content. In addition, prereading and postreading activities allow the teacher to prepare students for reading and assess their comprehension of the literature. Key words, concepts, and people who appear in the book and that relate to building a knowledge base are identified.

A variety of learning activities present ideas for extending learning. Reproducible student activity sheets are referred to by boldface title and page number for easy reference. The teacher-led activities and blackline master pages were designed to link the content of the book with core academic areas such as reading, spelling, mathematics, social studies, science, art, and the humanities.

Indigenous, or native, people play an important role in their country's history and culture. Unfortunately, many people grow up misinformed about the cultures, languages, and lifestyles of the people native to their country. Further, too few recognize or honor the achievements and contributions of these original inhabitants. This book will assist students in challenging stereotypes, gaining valuable background knowledge about Native Americans, and becoming aware of the answer to the question, "What are the influences of Native Americans on our past and present society and culture?"

Plains

Black Elk, A Man with a Vision

Author: Carol Greene

Publisher: Childrens Press, 1990.

Summary: This biography of Black Elk (1863-1950), a Sioux spiritual leader, tells the story of the conflict between the Sioux and the white people who came to their land. The book also recounts the role Black Elk and his vision played in helping the Sioux during a time of profound turmoil and change.

Prereading Activity:

Discuss with students the idea of a vision. Ask students what it means to "have a vision." Ask if they have ever "seen" something before it happened. Have students tell about their visions and what they think they meant.

Key Words, Concepts, and People:

- have a vision
- Ghost Dance
- peace
- Black Hills
- Wounded Knee
- Little Bighorn
- Wild West Show
- Great Spirit
- Crazy Horse

Postreading Discussion Questions:

1. Why did white people first come to the Black Hills in large numbers and want to take land from the Sioux? *(Gold was discovered in the Black Hills.)*

2. What was young Black Elk's vision? *(He had a vision of peace. Looking down on the world from a mountaintop, he saw a huge tree filled with flowers and a great tepee with a rainbow door and six grandfathers inside.)*

3. What happened to the Sioux after they lost the war with the white people and most of the buffalo were killed? *(The Sioux were herded together onto reservations where many people died from disease. Their supply of food and materials for shelter was gone.)*

4. Why did Black Elk join Buffalo Bill's Wild West Show and travel to Europe? *(He thought he might learn a way to help his people.)*

5. What is the Ghost Dance? *(It is a dance in which an Indian holy man encourages his people to help bring back the buffalo and Indians who have been killed and make the plains more like they were before the whites came.)*

6. When did Black Elk feel that his people's dream died? *(Their dreams died in 1890 at Wounded Knee, where many Sioux men, women, and children were massacred by white soldiers.)*

© Teacher Created Materials, Inc.   5   #476 Learning Through Literature—Native Americans

Plains

Black Elk, A Man with a Vision (cont.)

Learning Activities:

- **The Life of Black Elk (page 7)** Have students use the table to answer the questions that follow it. **Answers:** 1. 1873, 2. 3, 3. 19, 4. 19, 5. 1890, 6. 87
- **Buffalo (page 8)** Have students complete the chart. **Answers:** meat for food; hide for clothing, rugs, tepee covers, and strips for ropes; head for a mask; horns for sharp instruments, containers, utensils, and decorations; bones for tools, sewing, and toys; stomach as medicine and to make toys for children
- **Making Moccasins (page 9)** Tell students that most Native Americans, including the Sioux, wore moccasins and decorated them with beads and feathers. Send the directions home with students and invite them to bring their moccasins to school to share with the class. You may wish to bring in the materials and make moccasins as a class project.
- Have students draw a picture of a tepee on a separate sheet of paper. Have them decorate the outside of the tepee with pictures they think Indians might have painted or drawn onto the buffalo hides.

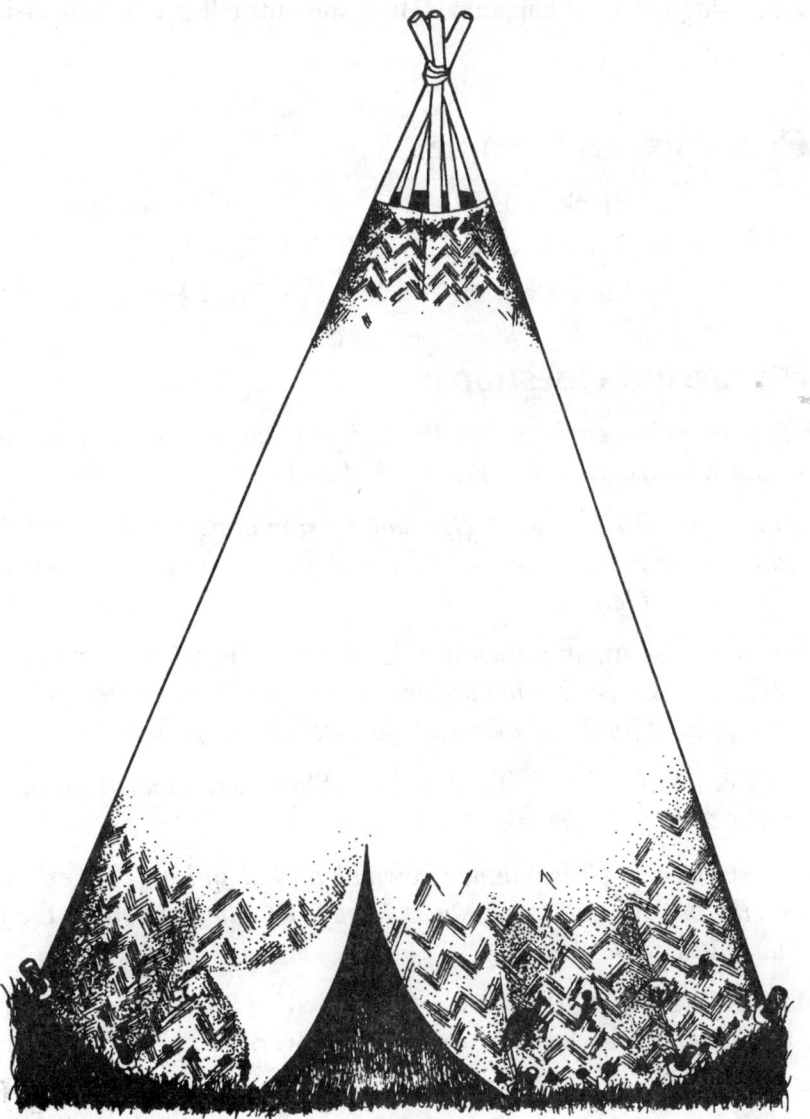

Plains

Name _____ Date _____

The Life of Black Elk

Answer the questions, using the table of dates important in Black Elk's life.

YEAR	DESCRIPTION
1863	Black Elk is born near the Little Powder River. His father is Black Elk, and his mother is White Cow Sees.
1873	Black Elk has a vision about peace and harmony in the world.
1876	A fierce battle breaks out between the whites and the Sioux at the Little Big Horn River.
1882	Black Elk becomes a medicine man.
1886–1889	Black Elk travels in Europe as part of a Wild West Show.
1890	The Sioux are massacred at the battle of Wounded Knee.
1931	Black Elk tells his life story to John Neihardt, who writes a book about him.
1950	Black Elk dies on Pine Ridge Reservation in South Dakota.

1. In what year did Black Elk have his first vision? _____
2. How many years did Black Elk travel in Europe? _____
3. How old was Black Elk when he became a medicine man? _____
4. How many years after telling his life story did Black Elk die? _____
5. In what year did Black Elk's vision die with the massacre at Wounded Knee?
   _____
6. How old was Black Elk when he died? _____

Plains

Name _____ Date _____

Buffalo

The buffalo was an important food and clothing source for the Plains Indians. They used all parts of the buffalo. In the boxes, write how the Plains Indians used the different parts of the buffalo.

The meat	
The hide	
The head	
The horns	
The bones	
The stomach	

#476 Learning Through Literature—Native Americans   8   © Teacher Created Materials, Inc.

Plains

Name _____ Date _____

Making Moccasins

Follow the steps listed below to make your own moccasins. Ask an older member of your family to help you when you handle the sharp things. Materials may be found at fabric or craft supply stores.

Materials:

sturdy fabric, such as denim or canvas; scissors; crayon or marker; straight pins; needle; heavy-duty thread; paper

Step 1: Make moccasin patterns by placing a pair of your shoes on paper and tracing around each shoe with a crayon or marker. Cut out the paper patterns.

Step 2: Fold the fabric in half and pin the paper patterns on it. Make fabric moccasin pieces by cutting around the patterns.

Step 3: Taking small stitches, sew around the edges of the fabric pieces.

Step 4: Make an opening for your foot by carefully cutting a hole in the top piece of fabric only. Start with a small hole and make it bigger a little at a time until your foot fits in it.

Step 5: Decorate your moccasins. Use fabric paint, sequins, beads or yarn. Bring them to class to share.

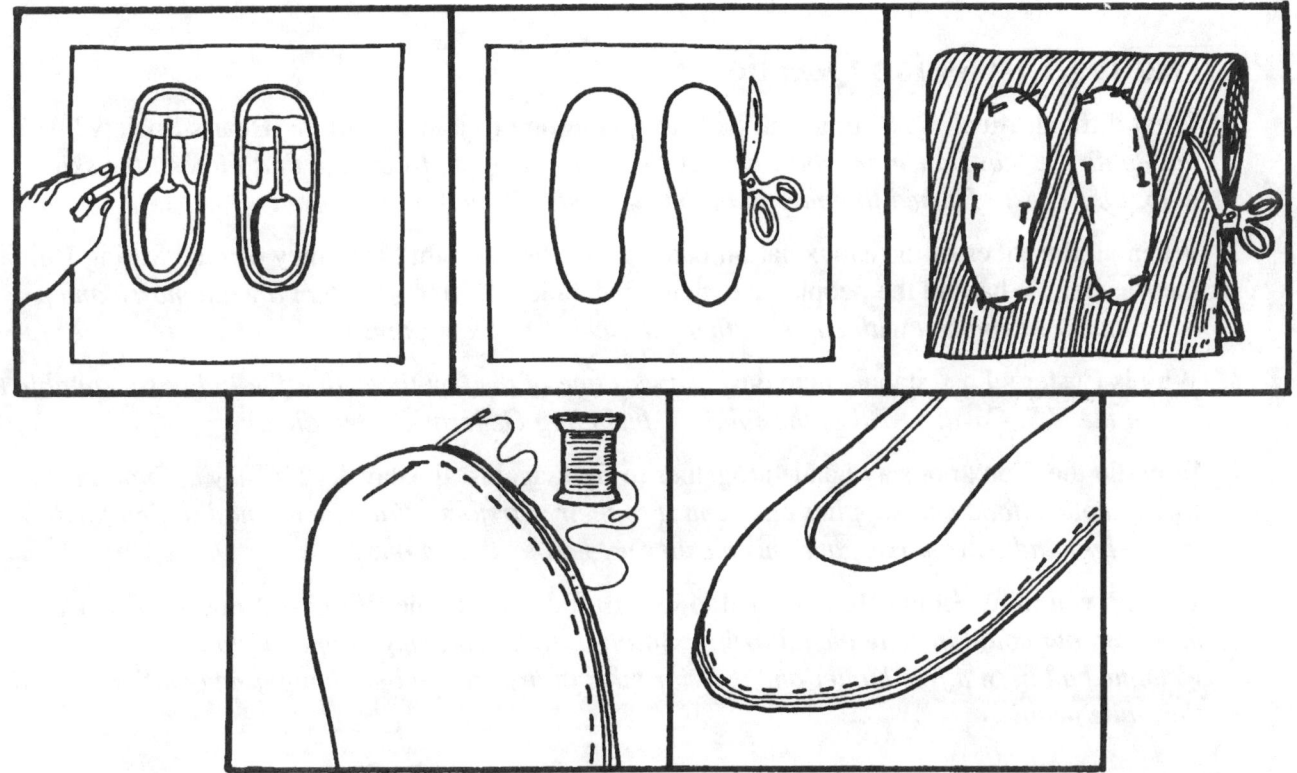

© Teacher Created Materials, Inc.   9   #476 *Learning Through Literature—Native Americans*

Plains

Sitting Bull (The Great American Series)

Author: Kathie Billingslea Smith

Illustrator: James Seward

Publisher: Simon & Schuster, Inc., 1987

Summary: This biography presents the story of Sitting Bull, the great Sioux chief who led the Indians to glory in the Battle of the Little Big Horn. It tells how Chief Sitting Bull came to symbolize the Native American.

Prereading Activity:

Ask children if they have heard the name Tatanka Yotanka. Then ask if they have ever heard of one of the greatest of all Native American chiefs, Sitting Bull. Tell them that Tatanka Yotanka means "Sitting Bull" in the Sioux language.

Key Words, Concepts, and People:

- counting coup
- Sun Dance
- Buffalo Bill
- war paint
- shaman
- reservation
- nomad
- Custer's Last Stand
- warbonnet

Postreading Discussion Questions:

1. What difficult ritual did Sitting Bull have to go through to join the Strong Hearts Society? *(He had to do the Sun Dance, in which he was tied to a high pole by a stick that pierced the skin across his chest. He had to dance until the stick pulled free.)*

2. When all the tribes of the Sioux nation banded together to fight back, they elected Sitting Bull as their leader. What did the people give their new leader? *(They gave him a white horse and a magnificent warbonnet with eagle feathers stretching to the ground.)*

3. Why is Custer's Last Stand so famous? *(It was one of the few times that the Indians were able to defeat the U.S. Cavalry. All of the soldiers, including General Custer, died.)*

4. Why did the Sioux not stay banded together to fight against the cavalry? *(They did not have a way to collect food and supplies and send it to their warriors. Each family had to find food for themselves and their horses, and this meant they had to spread out.)*

5. Why do you think Sitting Bull decided to join Buffalo Bill in the Wild West Show? *(Answers may vary but could include the following: Sitting Bull hated being cooped up on the reservation when he had been a free hunter and warrior most of his life, and he thought he could learn from the white people.)*

Plains

Sitting Bull (cont.)

Learning Activities:

- Rent the film *Dances with Wolves;* preview it first and show excerpts of it where the Sioux Plains Indians are speaking their language. Tell the students that people still use the native languages, although less than before. Explain to them that the subheadings are translations of the language. Play pieces of the film several times and ask students if they can learn any of the words.

- Show students pictures from the book and ask them to identify what animal parts were used to make. For example, one of the headdresses worn includes antlers from a deer, feathers from a bird, and hide from a buffalo.

- **Sitting Bull's War Bonnet (page 12)** When Sitting Bull was elected chief of all of the Sioux Plains Indians, he was given a war bonnet. Have students write on each feather something about Sitting Bull, then color the bonnet.

- Have students work with partners and write letters to the Bureau of Indian Affairs. Ask each pair to request different information about some aspect of Indian affairs today, such as ceremonies, festivals, or locations of reservations. Have students share with the class the information they receive. The address is Bureau of Indian Affairs, U.S. Department of the Interior, Washington, DC 20245.

- Discuss with students the shaman, or the religious and medical leader of a Native American tribe. Have students research the shaman's role in the different tribes. Create a chart showing the different roles the shaman filled in Native American society.

- **Becoming a Warrior (page 13)** Picture cues in boxes 1–3 show things Sitting Bull had to do to become a warrior. Have students draw in box 4 another thing they think would have been important for a Sioux Indian to do to prepare for being a warrior.

- Ask students to work in groups of three to discuss the procedures needed to become a member of the Strong Hearts Warriors. Ask student groups to develop their own group for women in the Sioux tribe, give this important new group a name, and describe the practices women would need to do to become a member. Let each of the student groups report on what they have developed.

- **Plains Indian Words (page 14)** Have students find the words listed and draw a ring around each of them. Remind students that words can run vertically, horizontally, and diagonally in the word search.

© Teacher Created Materials, Inc.   11   #476 Learning Through Literature—Native Americans

Plains

Name _____ Date _____

Sitting Bull's Warbonnet

On each feather, write a fact about Sitting Bull. One feather is done for you. Then color the warbonnet.

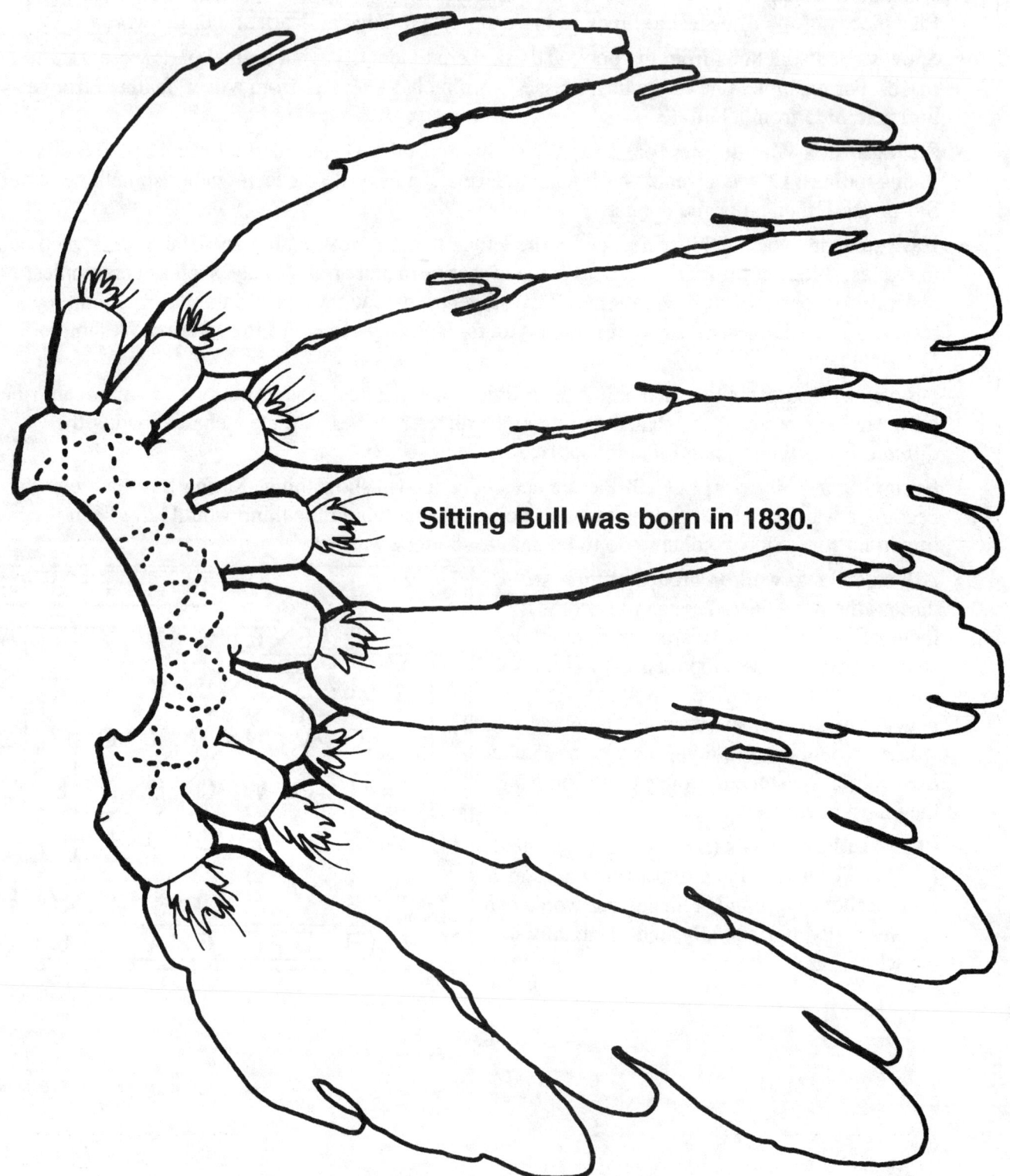

Sitting Bull was born in 1830.

Plains

Name _____ Date _____

Becoming a Warrior

Each picture shows one thing that Sitting Bull had to do to become a warrior. On the lines underneath the picture, describe what Sitting Bull is doing. In box 4, draw your own picture showing something you think would have been important for a Sioux Indian to do in order to prepare to be a warrior. Describe it on the lines under the box.

1. _____

2. _____

3. _____

4. _____

© Teacher Created Materials, Inc.　　　13　　　#476 Learning Through Literature—Native Americans

Plains

Name _____ Date _____

Plains Indian Words

Find the words listed and draw a circle around each.

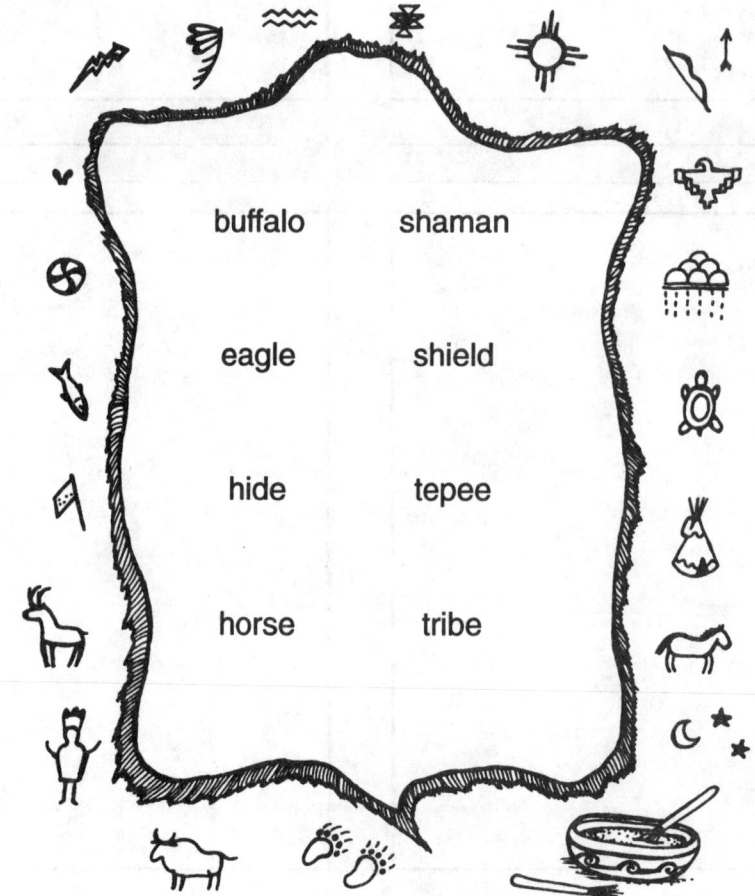

buffalo   shaman

eagle   shield

hide   tepee

horse   tribe

#476 Learning Through Literature—Native Americans   14   © Teacher Created Materials, Inc.

Plains

Sky Dogs

Author: Jane Yolen

Illustrator: Barry Moser

Publisher: Harcourt Brace Jovanovich, 1990

Summary: This book recounts the almost magical story of how horses first came to the Piegan, a band of Blackfoot Indians. Having horses greatly changed the lives of Native Americans.

Prereading Activity:

Have children imagine a time when Native Americans had only dogs to help pull their loads and had to hunt buffalo on foot. Discuss with students what the coming of horses must have meant to the Plains Indians.

Key Words, Concepts, and People:

- Old Man
- sacred herb
- council
- travois
- elk
- Kutani
- Sky Dogs
- coup
- Piegan

Postreading Discussion Questions:

1. When the Piegan first saw the strange beasts coming from the west, they were frightened. Why do you think they were afraid? *(Answers may vary.)*

2. Why do you think the Piegan called horses "Sky Dogs"? *(They pulled travois like dogs did, but they were much larger. The Piegan thought horses were a gift of the great spirit, the Old Man, so they must have come from the sky.)*

3. What were some of the other things that the Piegan felt were gifts from the Old Man? *(They believed the Old Man also sent them buffalo, antelope, and bighorn sheep.)*

4. Why do you think the men tried to feed the horses meat and to throw sticks for them to bring back? Did these things work? *(Answers may vary but could include the following: The Piegan really thought of horses as a kind of large dog. These things didn't work because horses do not eat meat or play by fetching sticks.)*

5. The name of the storyteller in the book is He-Who-Loves-Horses. What was his name in his native language? *("He-Who-Loves-Horses" is a translation into English of his name in his native language. This is like "Phillip" which is a name in English that means he-who-loves-horses. This comes from the Greek,* phil, *"loves," and* hip, *"horse.")*

© Teacher Created Materials, Inc.   15   #476 Learning Through Literature—Native Americans

Plains

Sky Dogs *(cont.)*

Learning Activities:

- One of the characters in the book is named He-Who-Loves-Horses. Explain to students that Native American adolescents were often given second names, which reflected their interests and skills. Have students think of a name they would like to have, based on their skills and interests. Ask each student to share with the class the name they have chosen and why.

- *Sky Dogs* begins: "My children, you ask how I came to be called He-Who-Loves-Horses, for now I sit in the tipi, and food is brought to me, and I do not ride the wind. Come close—there—there. Come close, and I will tell you." Discuss with students how they can tell from this excerpt that the person speaking is not young. Have students write their own beginning sentences from the perspective of a young person.

- Remind students that the warrior Flint Knife said, "I wish that white people had never come into my country." Discuss with students why they think he said this. With the class, generate a list of things white people did that harmed Flint Knife's people.

- **Poem (page 17)** An Osage Indian poem expresses how the Plains Indians felt about their land. Read the poem aloud with the class. Allow time for students to complete the activity sheet and then have volunteers share their impressions.

- **Hunting Buffalo (page 18)** The Crow were a Plains Indian people who were very good warriors and hunters. Even though they mostly hunted their buffalo by foot, they were very successful. Give students time to list other techniques that they think the Crow may have used to hunt buffalo. Have volunteers read their lists. **Additional Answers:** They wore buffalo skins so as not to frighten the buffalo as they got close to them; they stampeded buffalo herds over cliffs to kill or maim them.

- **Interview with He-Who-Loves-Horses (page 19)** Ask students to pretend that they are He-Who-Loves-Horses being interviewed by a reporter. Then have them think of a question and the answer for it.

Plains

Name _____ Date _____

Poem

Read the following poem written by an Osage Indian. On the lines below the poem, tell what you think the writer means.

A Person

I am a person never absent
from any important act,
Great Elk is the name I have taken.
When men hunt little animals
I always make them appear
to them. In the midst of each of the four
winds, I throw myself upon the earth.
I cleanse all the land of my anger. I throw myself and leave the
hairs of my body—these hairs I have
scattered so that animals may
appear in their midst, they are
the grasses of this earth. I have made the grasses
so the animals may appear
so you may live upon the earth,
upon the earth.

_____
_____
_____
_____
_____
_____
_____
_____

© Teacher Created Materials, Inc.   17   #476 Learning Through Literature—Native Americans

Plains

Name _____ Date _____

Hunting Buffalo

Below are two ways the Crow hunted buffalo. Remember that they did not have horses and that they mostly used bows, arrows, and hatchets. Then list some other ways the Crow could have hunted and killed the buffalo they needed for food and shelter.

Hunting Methods

1. They chose buffaloes that had strayed away from the main herd.

2. They wore animal skins, perhaps even buffalo skins, to fool the buffalo into thinking that they were harmless animals.

3. _____
_____
_____

4. _____
_____
_____

5. _____
_____
_____

6. _____
_____
_____

7. _____
_____
_____

Plains

Name _____ Date _____

Interview with He-Who-Loves-Horses

Pretend you are He-Who-Loves-Horses talking to a reporter. Answer the reporter's questions.

Reporter: How old are you?

He-Who-Loves-Horses: _____

Reporter: Tell me one of your favorite memories from living on the plains.

He-Who-Loves-Horses: _____
_____
_____

Reporter: What is one of the saddest things that has ever happened to you?

He-Who-Loves-Horses: _____
_____
_____

Reporter: Tell me about your family in the past and present.

He-Who-Loves-Horses: _____
_____
_____

Now write your own question and answer it.

Reporter: _____
_____

He-Who-Loves-Horses: _____
_____
_____

© Teacher Created Materials, Inc.　　19　　#476 Learning Through Literature—Native Americans

Plains

Cherokee Summer

Author: Diane Hoyt-Goldsmith

Photographer: Lawrence Migdale

Publisher: Holiday House, 1993

Summary: This book traces the ancestry and culture of a young Cherokee girl living in Okay, Oklahoma. The story imparts a real sense of the strong traditions that have given the Cherokee a sense of identity and pride.

Prereading Activity:

Read aloud the acknowledgments at the beginning of the book. Then discuss with students the authenticity of the book. Brainstorm with students what they expect to learn from reading this book.

Key Words, Concepts, and People:

- full-blood
- stomp dance
- hog fry
- blowgun
- clan
- shackles
- crowded
- fry bread

Postreading Discussion Questions:

1. Do you think the Cherokee have been treated fairly? Why or why not? *(Answers may vary.)*

2. Why was the road Bridget's ancestors traveled called the "Trail of Tears"? *(Answers may vary but could include: It is called that because many people died along the way.)*

3. Why don't the Cherokee of Oklahoma live on reservations like many other Native Americans? *(Answers may vary but could include that the Cherokee still own their own land.)*

4. The Cherokee Nation is the second largest group of Native Americans in the United States. What Indian nation is the largest? *(The Navajo Nation is the largest.)* What contributions have the Cherokee made that are helpful to us today? *(Answers may vary.)*

5. What is meant by being a "full-blood" Cherokee? *(Both parents are Cherokee.)* What is meant by being a "mixed-blood" Cherokee? *(One parent is Cherokee and the other is not.)*

6. Would you like to spend a summer with Bridget? Why or why not? *(Answers may vary.)*

Plains

Cherokee Summer (cont.)

Learning Activities:

- **Making History (page 22)** Discuss with students the many historical events that took place in this story and list them on the chalkboard. Assign pairs or small groups a particular event and ask them to complete the worksheet. Display the completed worksheets in the order in which they occurred. Have teams present their event in creative ways—a skit, puppet show, overhead presentation—to parents or other classes.

- One of the events Bridget enjoyed during her Cherokee summer was the Hog Fry Dinner. Many families and cultural groups enjoy traditional celebrations. Divide the students into small groups and ask them to share such traditions in their families.

- Read books that introduce different Indian tribes, such as *Sitting Bull* by Jane Fliescher (Sioux) and *The Spider, the Cave, and the Pottery Bowl* by Eleanor Clymer (Hopi). Have children compare and contrast these books with *Cherokee Summer*. Talk about characters, setting, story line, theme, and tone. Ask children to choose their favorite stories and tell why they like them best.

- Bridget enjoys doing the stomp dance with her family and friends. Allow children to experiment with Native American dance movements. Suggested resources include the book and record *Dance-A-Story About the Brave Hunter* by Paul and Anne Barlin (Ginn and Co., 1965), musical selections from "Songs of Earth, Water, Fire, and Sky" on *Music of the American Indians* (New World Records, 1965), *Authentic Indian Dances and Folklore,* by Michigan Chippewa Chiefs (available from Kimbo Educational Records, P.O. Box 246, Deal, NJ 07723).

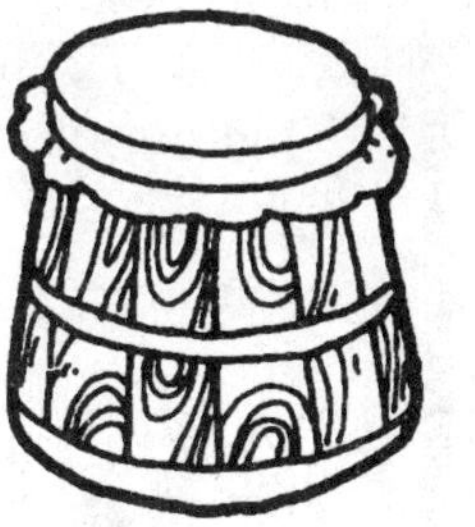

- **What We Should Know About the Cherokee (page 23)** Ask students to decide what they think is important that everyone should know about the Cherokee. Invite your principal in for a sharing session.

- **Compare and Contrast (page 24)** Discuss with students how their lives are similar to and different from Bridget's. Assign the activity sheet.

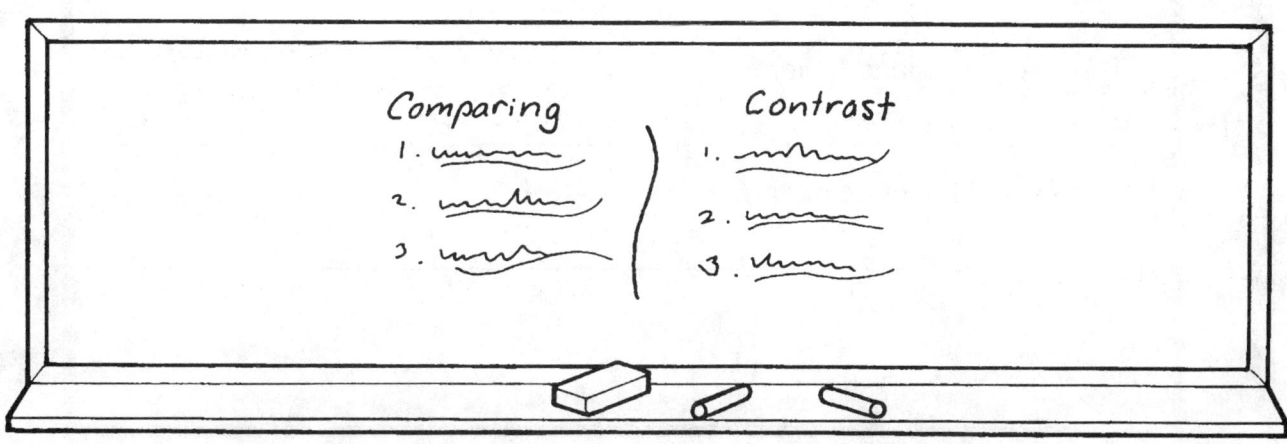

© *Teacher Created Materials, Inc.* 21 #476 *Learning Through Literature—Native Americans*

Plains

Name _____ Date _____

Making History

Choose one of the historical events described in *Cherokee Summer*. On the lines, write about the event you chose.

This is what happened
_____

This event happened on this date or during this period
_____

This event happened because
_____
_____

This event is important because
_____
_____

This event makes us feel
_____

This event could have been made better by
_____
_____

This event happened after
_____

This event happened before
_____

#476 Learning Through Literature—Native Americans © Teacher Created Materials, Inc.

Plains

Name _____ Date _____

What We Should Know About the Cherokee

Now that you have finished reading *Cherokee Summer*, what would you want all Americans to know about the Cherokee. Answer the following questions and then write a paragraph using your information. Use the lines below.

What one thing about the Cherokee would you choose to tell all Americans?
_____
_____

Why is it important for all Americans to know this?
_____
_____
_____
_____
_____
_____
_____
_____

What is the best way to tell other Americans about this?
_____
_____
_____
_____
_____
_____
_____
_____
_____

Plains

Name _____ Date _____

Compare and Contrast

Draw a picture or write a sentence in the box to show how your life compares with Bridget's.

Bridget and I both do this:	**Bridget does this, but I do not:**
Bridget does this, and I would like to do it, too:	**Bridget does this, and I am glad I do not have to do it:**

#476 Learning Through Literature—Native Americans　　24　　© Teacher Created Materials, Inc.

Plains

Where the Buffaloes Begin

Author: Olaf Baker

Illustrator: Stephen Gammell

Publisher: Viking Childrens Books, 1989

Summary: For as long as anyone could remember, Nawa, the wise man, had told his people of the Great Plains that the buffalo had their beginnings in the strange lake to the south. According to the legend, an adventuresome young boy named Little Wolf sets off to find the buffalo. He succeeds, and the buffalo help him save his people from death at the hands of their enemies, the Assiniboins.

Prereading Activity:

Read aloud to students the book's prologue. Explain that it is the introduction to an Indian legend that has been handed down through the generations from storyteller to storyteller. Tell students that a legend is often about a person who does great things. Ask students to consider, as they read, whether the legend of Little Wolf could have really happened or not.

Key Words, Concepts, and People:

- graze
- buffalo
- stampede
- antelope
- dismounted
- ambush
- tepees
- coyote

Postreading Discussion Questions:

1. Do you think Little Wolf did the right thing? Why or why not? *(Answers may vary.)*

2. How did Little Wolf know where to find the lake? *(Answers may vary.)*

3. Why do you think the buffalo did not hurt Little Wolf? *(Answers may vary.)*

4. What would have happened to Little Wolf and his people if the buffaloes had not stampeded the enemies? *(They may have been killed.)*

5. How do you think Little Wolf was treated by his people after the event? *(Answers may vary.)*

6. Do you believe that the legend of Little Wolf and the buffaloes might actually have happened? Why or why not? *(Answers may vary.)*

© Teacher Created Materials, Inc. 25 #476 Learning Through Literature—Native Americans

Plains

Where the Buffaloes Begin (cont.)

Learning Activities:

- The buffalo once appeared on one of our coins, the nickel. These coins have become collectors items. Have students ask their families and friends if they or anyone they know collects buffalo nickels. Have students invite that person to share his/her collection with the class.

- Buffaloes were once a source for food and clothing for the people of the plains. Native Americans used almost every part of the buffalo they killed. White men slaughtered buffalo for their horns and hides only; they left most of the buffalo on the plains to rot. Because of the whites' greed and waste, the buffalo became endangered nearly to the point of extinction. Have volunteers research the history of the buffalo and report back to the class.

- Read other Native American tales, myths, and legends such as Paul Goble's *The Girl Who Loved Wild Horses* or *The Gift of the Sacred Dog*. Compare and contrast these stories with *Where the Buffaloes Begin*.

- Olaf Baker was able to retell this legend and write other stories because of his many years of travel throughout the West, particularly in the territories of the Blackfoot Indians. Divide the students into groups. Provide resources and ample time for each group to research a different Indian nation. Encourage students to learn about the lifestyles (homes, clothing, celebrations, food, crafts) of these people during the early years of our country's history. Have each group share its research with the class.

- **Word Search (page 27)** Have students find and circle words from the story, define them, and write a sentence using each word. **Suggested Definitions:** dismounted—got off a horse; antelope—a swift, long-horned animal that resembles a deer; coyote—a wolflike animal; teepee—cone-shaped tent made of skin or bark; stampede—a sudden rush of a herd of animals; buffalo—an oxlike animal; ambush—a surprise attack made from a hidden position

- **Little Wolf's Character (page 28)** Ask students to provide some adjectives that best describe Little Wolf. Write them on the chalkboard. Have students tell why they think these words apply to Little Wolf. Assign the activity sheet.

Plains

Name_____Date_____

Word Search

In the word search below, find the following words:

graze	teepees	dismounted	stampede
antelope	buffalo	coyote	ambush

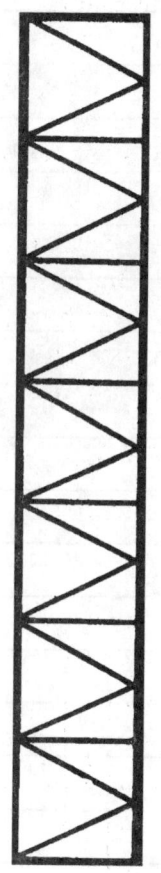
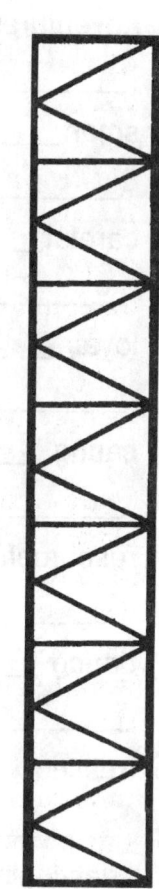

```
P O I U Y T R E W M B
M T U P A P A U S A D
D O F G M J A L K F E
S T A M P E D E M A G
P E N N R M P U G T O
A E T F A A J E R U J
R P E C B U F F A L O
E E L O N I T O Z P M
U E O I K L H D E T N
Q W P A M B U S H M P
F S E T H E A F E A Q
E S D C O Y O T E N R
K Z M A U I A J A U S
E D I S M O U N T E D
```

All these words are found in *Where the Buffaloes Begin*. Using the book and other sources, look up the definition of each word. Write the word, the definition, and a sentence using the word. Use the back of the page to complete all eight words. One is done for you.

Word: *graze*

Definition: *to feed on various grasses and plants*

Sentence: *The buffaloes liked to graze in the fields.*

© Teacher Created Materials, Inc.   27   #476 Learning Through Literature—Native Americans

Plains

Name _____ Date _____

Little Wolf's Character

Below are 10 adjectives that describe Little Wolf's character. For each adjective, describe one incident from the story that best shows how that trait fits Little Wolf. For number 11, choose your own word and incident from the story that describe Little Wolf.

1. brave _____
_____

2. adventuresome _____
_____

3. smart _____
_____

4. careful _____
_____

5. loyal _____
_____

6. caring _____
_____

7. resourceful _____
_____

8. daring _____
_____

9. trusting _____
_____

10. questioning _____
_____

11. _____
_____

Of all these traits, which do you feel is the most important for a person to have or to acquire?
_____
_____

Why?
_____
_____

#476 Learning Through Literature—Native Americans © Teacher Created Materials, Inc.

Plains

Her Seven Brothers

Author: Paul Goble

Illustrator: Paul Goble

Publisher: Bradbury Press, 1988

Summary: There once was a young girl whose embroidery was so beautiful that people believed she understood the spirits. After she disappeared to go live with her brothers (whom no one else had ever seen), the chief of the Buffalo Nation demanded that the girl return. This story tells the Cheyenne legend of how the Big Dipper was created.

Prereading Activity:

Show the students the cover of the book and read aloud the title. Ask students to predict what they think the story will be about. On a piece of poster board, write the students' predictions. Tell them that at the end of the story they will see whether their predictions were correct.

Key Words, Concepts, and People:

- embroidery
- moccasins
- bellowed
- tipi
- porcupine quills
- spirits
- yearling
- immensity

Postreading Discussion Questions:

1. If you were the girl's mother, would you have allowed her to go look for her brothers? Why or why not? *(Answers may vary.)*

2. What might have happened to the girl if she hadn't found her brothers or if they hadn't wanted her to live with them? *(Answers may vary.)*

3. Why do you think the Buffalo People wanted the little girl back? *(Answers may vary.)*

4. Which character do you think was the bravest? Why? *(Answers may vary.)*

5. What would have happened if the little brother hadn't had magic powers? *(Answers may vary.)*

6. Could any of this story actually have happened? If so, what parts? *(Answers may vary.)*

© Teacher Created Materials, Inc. 29 #476 Learning Through Literature—Native Americans

Plains

Her Seven Brothers (cont.)

Learning Activities:

- **Decorating Indian Clothing (page 31)** Read the note from Paul Goble in the beginning of the book in which he describes his illustrations. Next, look through the book again, paying careful attention to Goble's artistry in re-creating the beautiful designs. Ask students to decorate or create a pair of Indian moccasins and a shirt decorated with designs that relate to the story *Her Seven Brothers*. Allow time to share.

- **Agree or Disagree (page 32)** Discuss with the students that they may not always agree with what the author writes in a book. Have students complete the activity sheet in class. Allow time for students to debate their answers.

- Discuss with students that this story offers an explanation of how the Big Dipper was created. Show students an illustration of what the Big Dipper looks like—four stars forming a bowl and three stars forming the handle of a dipper. Encourage the students to find the Big Dipper in the night sky. Ask them to find the North Star and the tiny star they read about in *Her Seven Brothers*.

- On a piece of poster board, create a replica of an Indian campsite as shown in the book. Have students volunteer to make a part of the campsite, such as a tipi, campfire, animals, and so on, and place it on the poster board.

- **Could It Happen? (page 33)** Discuss with the class the difference between possible and impossible, reallife and fantasy. Assign the worksheet and go over it in class, asking students to give reasons for their decisions.

- Gather and read other books written by Paul Goble. Have students compare the illustrations and the stories in different books. This is a list of suggested books:

Star Boy
The Gift of the Sacred Dog
Death of the Iron Horse
The Girl Who Loved Wild Horses
Beyond the Ridge
Buffalo Woman
Dream Wolf
I Sing for the Animals
Crow Chief: A Plains Indian Story
Iktomi and the Berries

Name _____ Date _____

Plains

Decorating Indian Clothing

Decorate the moccasins and shirt with designs that relate to the story *Her Seven Brothers*.

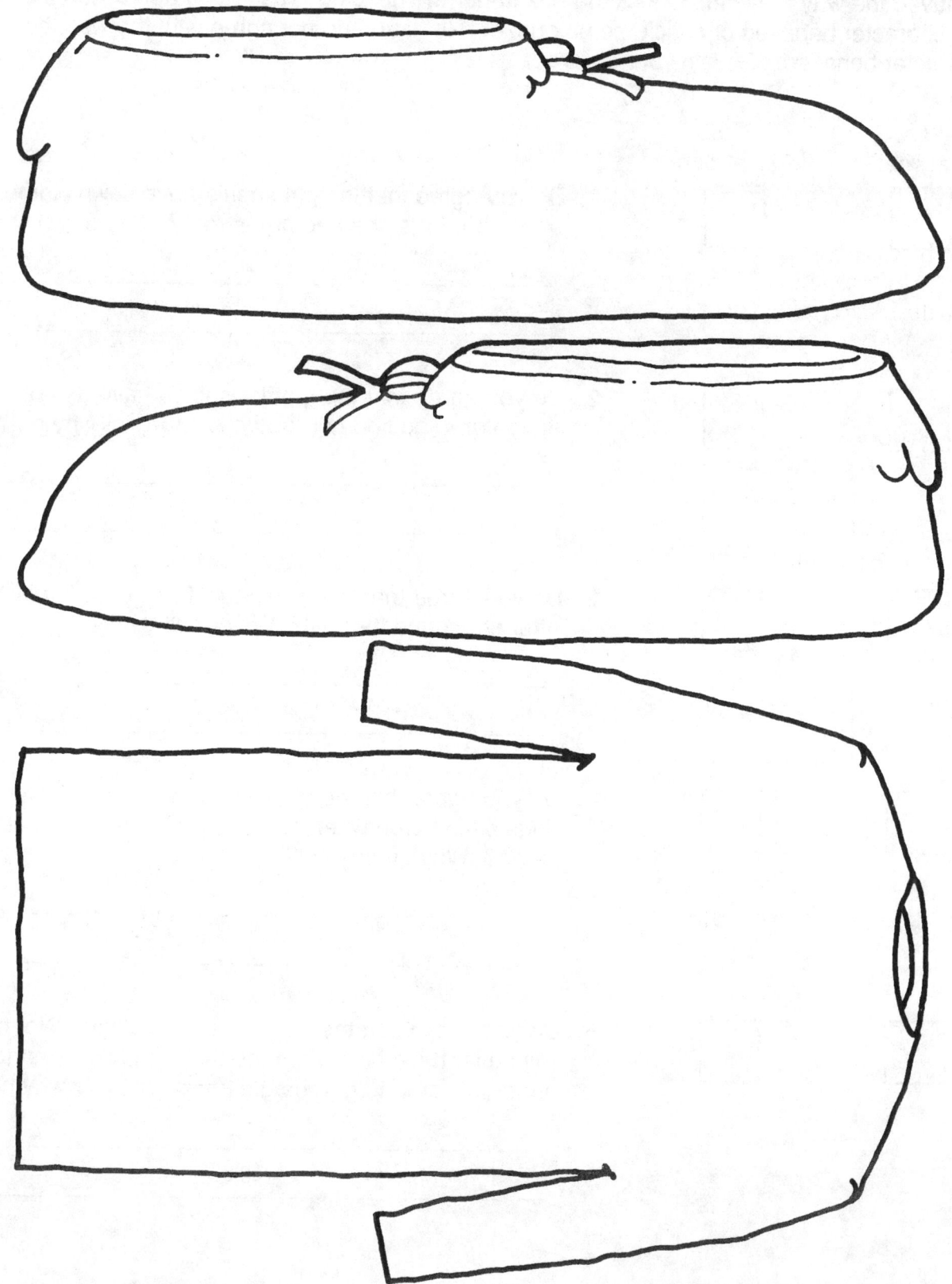

© *Teacher Created Materials, Inc.* 31 #476 *Learning Through Literature—Native Americans*

Plains

Name _____ Date _____

Agree or Disagree

Read each statement below and decide whether you think the characters should have behaved the way they did. Check the box under the heading "Yes" if you agree with the way the character behaved or check the box under "No" if you do not agree with the way the character behaved. Explain your answer.

Yes,   **No,**
I agree.   **I do not agree.**

☐   ☐   1. Do you agree that the girl should have sewn clothes for seven brothers she had never met? Why or why not?

_____
_____

☐   ☐   2. Do you agree that the mother should have allowed her daughter to go find her brothers? Why or why not?

_____
_____

☐   ☐   3. Do you agree that the girl should have gone on alone after she found the trail? Why or why not?

_____
_____

☐   ☐   4. Do you agree that the girl should have sent her two dogs back home when she got to the seven brothers' camp? Why or why not?

_____
_____

☐   ☐   5. Do you agree that the boy should have said, "No, he will never have her" when the three buffalo came to the brothers' camp to get the girl back? Why or why not?

_____
_____

#476 Learning Through Literature—Native Americans   © Teacher Created Materials, Inc.

Plains

Name _____ Date _____

Could It Happen?

Some things in *Her Seven Brothers* could happen in real life. Some things could not happen. Read the following list of events from the story. Decide whether each thing could or could not happen and mark your answer in either column. Explain your decision on the line following.

	Could Happen	Could Not Happen
1. The brothers and the girl jump onto a star-prairie. _____	☐	☐
2. The Big Dipper is really the girl and her brothers. _____	☐	☐
3. The tree grows taller as the little boy shoots an arrow into the sky. _____	☐	☐
4. The girl sees seven brothers in her mind. _____	☐	☐
5. Dogs pull carts or sleds. _____	☐	☐
6. The land is green and beautiful with flowers. _____	☐	☐
7. The girl sends her dogs back home. _____	☐	☐
8. A storyteller tells a story by a campfire. _____	☐	☐
9. Parents are proud of their daughter. _____	☐	☐

© Teacher Created Materials, Inc. 33 #476 Learning Through Literature—Native Americans

Plains

First Came the Indians

Author: M.J. Wheeler

Illustrator: James Houston

Publisher: Antheneum, 1983

Summary: This book describes the social (belief system) and material (food, clothing, and shelter) culture of six Native American tribes: Iroquois, Creek, Chippewa, Sioux, Makah, and Hopi.

Prereading Activity:

Show the students the cover and read aloud the title of the book. Then ask the students to share what they know about Native Americans (Indians). Ask them to name tribes that they have heard about. (Note: The tribes discussed in this book include tribes from the Plains, Southwest, and Northwest regions.)

Key Words, Concepts, and People:

- longhouse
- settlers
- tipis
- forest spirit
- wigwam
- grasslands
- brick bark

Postreading Discussion Questions:

1. Which Indian tribe did you find to be the most interesting? Explain. *(Answers may vary.)*

2. What do you think is the major contribution of the Indian culture to America? Explain. *(Answers may vary.)*

3. How are the Indian tribes described in this book similar and how they are different? *(Answers may vary.)*

4. How do you think the different tribes get along with each other? Are they friends? *(Answers may vary.)*

5. In what ways are today's Native Americans the same or different compared to their ancestors? *(Answers may vary.)*

6. If you could choose to join a tribe, which would you choose? Why? *(Answers may vary.)*

Plains

First Came the Indians *(cont.)*

Learning Activities:

- **K-W-L (page 36)** Before reading, have students work in pairs to complete 1-2 on the K-W-L activity sheet. Students will assess what they know and what they want to learn. After reading, have them complete number 3—what they have learned. Allow time to share these worksheets.
- Divide the class into six groups and have each group choose one of the tribes discussed in this book. Have students research their tribe and present what they have found to the class in an interesting way.
- **Indian Home (page 37)** Discuss the various types of habitats/homes in which Indians lived. For more suggestions and illustrations of tipis, bring to the classroom *Gifts of the Sacred Dog* and *Buffalo Woman*, both by Paul Goble. *Where Indians Live: American Indian Houses* by Nashone (Sierra Oaks, 1989) would also be a useful book for students to use during this project. Hand out copies of the activity sheet and allow students to share their drawings with the class.

- Many of the tribes had different games the children played. Obtain a copy of *Book of American Indian Games* by Allen and Paulette MacFarlan (Dover, Inc., 1985) and help students play some of the games.
- Obtain the ethnological map called "Indians in North America" (National Geographic Society, 1982) and display it on a wall. As the different Indian tribes are introduced, locate on the map the places where they have lived and/or currently live.
- Take the class on a field trip to a local museum that provides a display of Native American artifacts. Ask children to draw pictures and take notes about things they see while in the museum. When you return to the classroom, ask students to illustrate the display they found to be most interesting and write a brief paragraph describing it. Compile the papers into a class booklet entitled "Our Trip to the Museum."
- **Send a Telegram (page 38)** Brainstorm with the class about information the Indians could have used to help them. Have each students write a telegram to one of the Indian tribes. Allow time for all students to share their messages.

Plains

Name _____Date _____

K-W-L

Complete numbers 1 and 2 before reading *First Came the Indians;* answer number 3 after you have read it.

1. **K**—What I **K**now about Indians (Native Americans)

2. **W**—What I **W**ant to find out about Indians

3. **L**—What I **L**earned and still need to learn about Indians

#476 Learning Through Literature—Native Americans © Teacher Created Materials, Inc.

Plains

Name _____ Date _____

Indian Home

Select one of the Indian tribes' habitat/home discussed in *First Came the Indians* **and draw it below. Write the name of the tribe whose home you have drawn.**

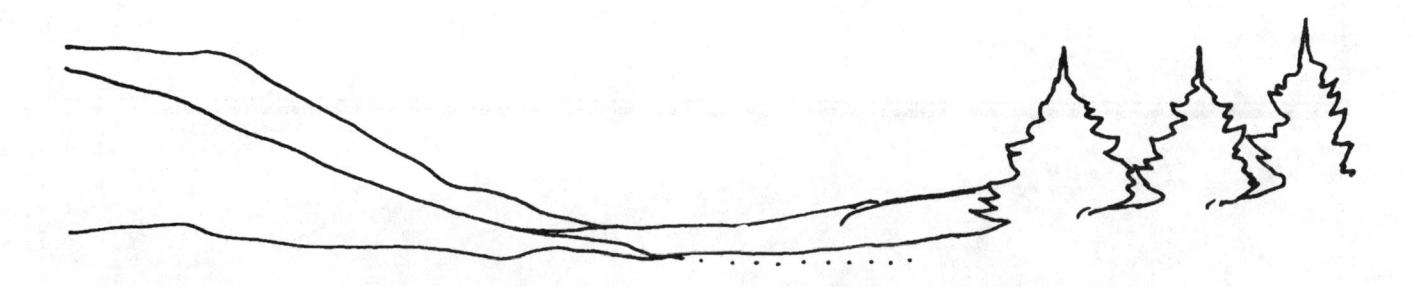

© Teacher Created Materials, Inc. 37 #476 Learning Through Literature—Native Americans

Plains

Name _____ Date _____

Send a Telegram

Write a telegram of 25 words or less to send important information to one of the Indian tribes discussed in *First Came the Indians*.

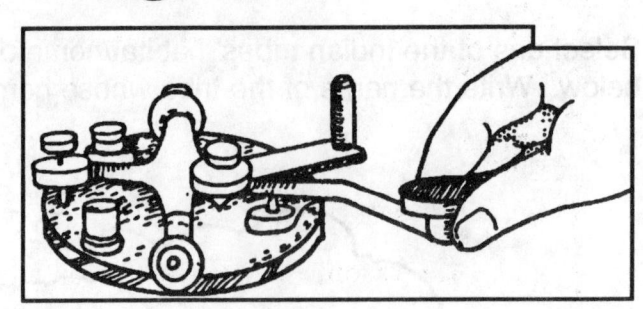

TELEGRAM

To:

From:

Message:

Plains

Buffalo Woman

Author: Paul Goble

Illustrator: Paul Goble

Publisher: Bradbury Press, 1984

Summary: Just when a young hunter is about to kill a buffalo, it turns into a woman. He and the woman fall in love, marry, and have a son. His family rejects her, so she and her son go back to the Buffalo Nation. The young man follows them and has to pass several tests of strength before he can join her family.

Prereading Activity:

Read the paragraph in the beginning of the book (under "for Marco"). Discuss with the class the idea that humans and buffaloes are related. Ask students to think about this idea as they read the story.

Key Words, Concepts, and People:

- magpies
- cockle-burr
- yearlings
- bowstring
- sagebrush
- bellowed
- tipi
- trample

Postreading Discussion Questions:

1. Did the young man know the woman he married was once a buffalo? Explain. *(Answers may vary.)*

2. Why didn't the young man's family like the young woman he married? *(Answers may vary but could include that they thought her ways were different and that she was like an animal.)*

3. Describe the young man and young woman. *(Answers may vary.)*

4. Do you think the young man did the right thing by following his wife and son even though he was in danger? Explain. *(Answers may vary.)*

5. How did the son make sure his father would know him and his mother when mixed in with the other buffaloes? *(He would flick his left ear and the mother would have a cockle-burr on her back.)* Do you think this was fair to the old bull who set up this test? Why or why not? *(Answers may vary.)*

6. Do you think the Buffalo Nation will continue to accept the young man as one of them, or will they eventually reject him as the young man's people did his wife and son? *(Answers may vary.)*

© Teacher Created Materials, Inc.   39   #476 Learning Through Literature—Native Americans

Plains

Buffalo Woman (cont.)

Learning Activities:

- **Character Traits (page 41)** Discuss the qualities of the characters in *Buffalo Woman*. Have students complete the activity sheet.
- **Write a Cinquain Poem (page 42)** Introduce the following outline and example of a cinquain poem by writing it on the chalkboard. Then ask students to write their own poems.

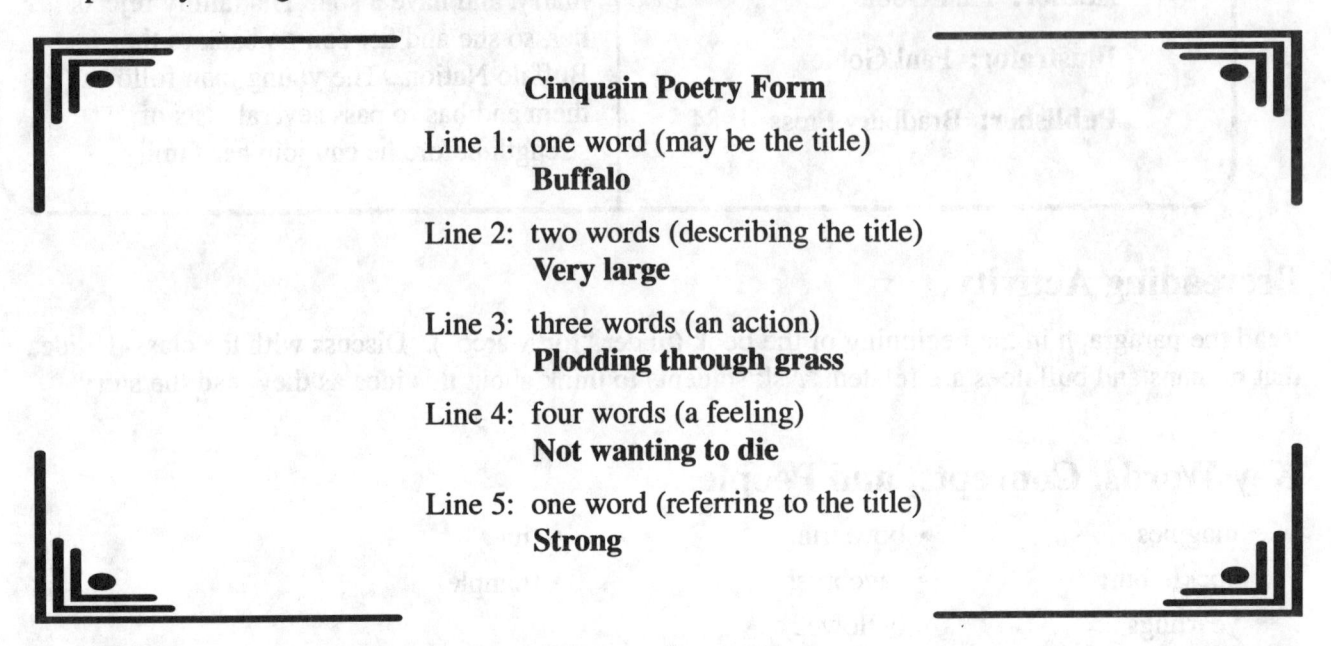

    Cinquain Poetry Form

    Line 1: one word (may be the title)
    Buffalo

    Line 2: two words (describing the title)
    Very large

    Line 3: three words (an action)
    Plodding through grass

    Line 4: four words (a feeling)
    Not wanting to die

    Line 5: one word (referring to the title)
    Strong

    Allow time to share poems and illustrations.

- Discuss with students that bows and arrows were the Native Americans' major tools for hunting and protecting themselves. They made bows from yew and other hard woods. They often decorated their bows. Arrows were made from rocks. Provide an opportunity (museum or local collectors) for the students to see what a typical bow and arrow would be like.
- **My Tipi (page 43)** Discuss how the young woman carried a tipi (tepee/tent) with her as she traveled back to the Buffalo Nation. Allow time for the students to look at the designs on the tipi in *Buffalo Woman* and encourage them to do further research on tipis. Then ask them to create a tipi and explain their designs. Note: You may want to create a real tipi in the classroom by dropping a sheet over a frame or card table. The book *Dancing Tepees—Poems of American Indian Youth* by Virginia Driving Hawk Sneve (Holiday House, 1989) provides good illustrations and designs.
- Invite the class to assist you in collecting books that relate to buffaloes, such as:

    Where the Buffaloes Begin by Olaf Baker (Viking Children's Books, 1989) and
    Iktomi and the Buffalo Skull by Paul Goble (Orchard Books, 1991).

- Have the class write a sequel to *Buffalo Woman*. What will happen now that the young man has become one of the Buffalo Nation? What would happen if sometime afterward he encountered his original tribe?

Name _____

Date _____

Character Traits

Below is a list of characters from *Buffalo Woman*. Check the qualities that each character has.

Character	kind	strong	mean	brave	persistent	courageous	clever	friendly	smart
young man									
young woman									
son									
old bull									
young man's people									

Select one character: _____

Describe how the story showed this character's qualities: _____

_____

_____

Plains

© Teacher Created Materials, Inc. 41 #476 Learning Through Literature—Native Americans

Plains

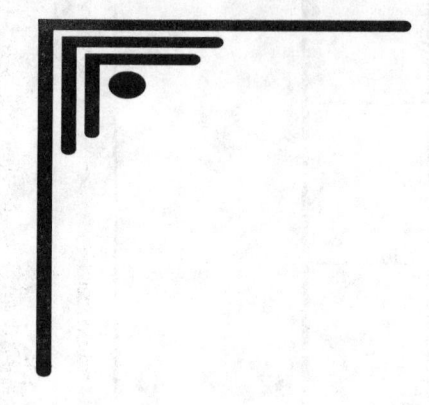

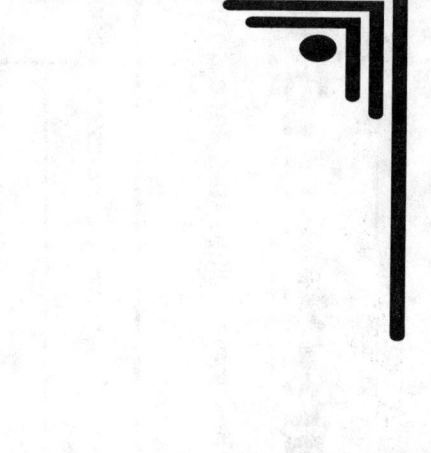

Name_____ Date _____

Write a Cinquain Poem

Follow the outline below to write in the frame below your own cinquain poem about the story of the buffalo woman. Draw a picture about your cinquain poem.

Line 1: one word (may be the title)

Line 2: two words (describe the title)

Line 3: three words (an action)

Line 4: four words (a feeling)

Line 5: one word (refers to the title)

Plains

Name _____ Date _____

My Tipi

Draw a tipi. Put designs that have some meaning to you on it.

Why did you choose the designs you did? _____
_____

Would you like to live in a tipi? Why or why not? _____
_____
_____

Plains

Iktomi and the Buffalo Skull

Author Paul Goble

Illustrator: Paul Goble

Publisher: Orchard Books, 1991

Summary: *Iktomi and the Buffalo Skull* is a Plains Indian story about the Indian trickster, Iktomi, and how he interrupts a powwow of Mouse People. In doing so, he gets his head stuck in a buffalo skull and suffers ridicule and suffering.

Prereading Activity:

Read aloud "About Iktomi" in the beginning of the story and ask students to discuss their thoughts. What is a trickster? What kind of trouble will Iktomi get into? What do you think the purpose of such a story is?

Key Words, Concepts, and People:

- lariats
- whack
- moccasins
- skull
- bashed
- ravines
- narrow bones
- powwow

Postreading Discussion Questions:

1. Describe Iktomi. Do you think people in his village liked him? Why or why not? *(Answers may vary.)*

2. Do you think Iktomi deserved to get stuck in the buffalo skull? Why or why not? *(Answers may vary.)*

3. Why do you think Iktomi was going to see his girlfriend in the next village when he was already married? *(Answers may vary.)*

4. Why did Iktomi's horse throw him off? *(Answers may vary but could include that he kicked him too hard and was rude to him.)*

5. How did the people in his camp feel when they saw Iktomi wearing a buffalo skull? *(They were terrified.)*

6. How do you feel about the way Iktomi's wife treated him? *(Answers may vary.)*

Plains

Iktomi and the Buffalo Skull (cont.)

Learning Activities:

- **Compound Words (page 46)** There are many compound words in *Iktomi and the Buffalo Skull*. Give several examples of compound words—dollhouse, ballgame, baseball, someone. Ask the students to tell compound words they know. Assign the activity sheet.

- **Where Iktomi Lived (page 47)** Discuss how people live in different types of homes and environments. Discuss Iktomi's environment with the class and have them complete the activity sheet.

- Assign students different parts of the story to dramatize. Allow time for preparation and rehearsal; then invite another class to come to see the play *Iktomi and the Buffalo Skull*.

- **Reading a Picture (page 48)** Have students complete the activity sheet in class. Allow time for students to share their interpretations.

- Paul Goble, the author of *Iktomi and the Buffalo Skull*, wrote a series of Iktomi stories—*Iktomi and the Boulder, Iktomi and the Berries, Iktomi and the Ducks*. Gather these books and allow students time to read them. Then create discussion groups in which the students compare and contrast these books.

- Iktomi lived in a camp or village. Have students create a Native American village. First, visit the library or bring in books depicting life in a village. Then provide students with construction paper, glue, crayons, markers, clay, scissors, and other materials. If possible, have them gather leaves, twigs, and grass from outside. Have children work cooperatively in planning and constructing the village. When the project is finished, display it in the classroom.

© Teacher Created Materials, Inc.   45   #476 Learning Through Literature—Native Americans

Plains

Name_____Date_____

Compound Words

There are many compound words in *Iktomi and the Buffalo Skull*. A compound word is one that is made by putting two words together. Put the words below together and write the compound word on the line.

war + bonnet = _____

cotton + wood = _____

no + where = _____

girl + friend = _____

no + body = _____

him + self = _____

pow + wow = _____

Use the compound words from above to complete the following sentences.

1. "_____ loves me," said Iktomi.

2. Iktomi was proud of his beautiful _____.

3. Iktomi went to the village to see his _____.

4. That is a _____ tree.

5. He was _____ to be seen.

6. Iktomi talked to _____.

7. Iktomi could hear the sounds of a _____.

Write five other compound words you know.

_____
_____
_____
_____
_____

#476 Learning Through Literature—Native Americans   46   © Teacher Created Materials, Inc.

Plains

Name_____ Date_____

Where Iktomi Lived

In each box below, draw one thing about the place where Iktomi lived that is different from where you live. You can get ideas from the story and its pictures.

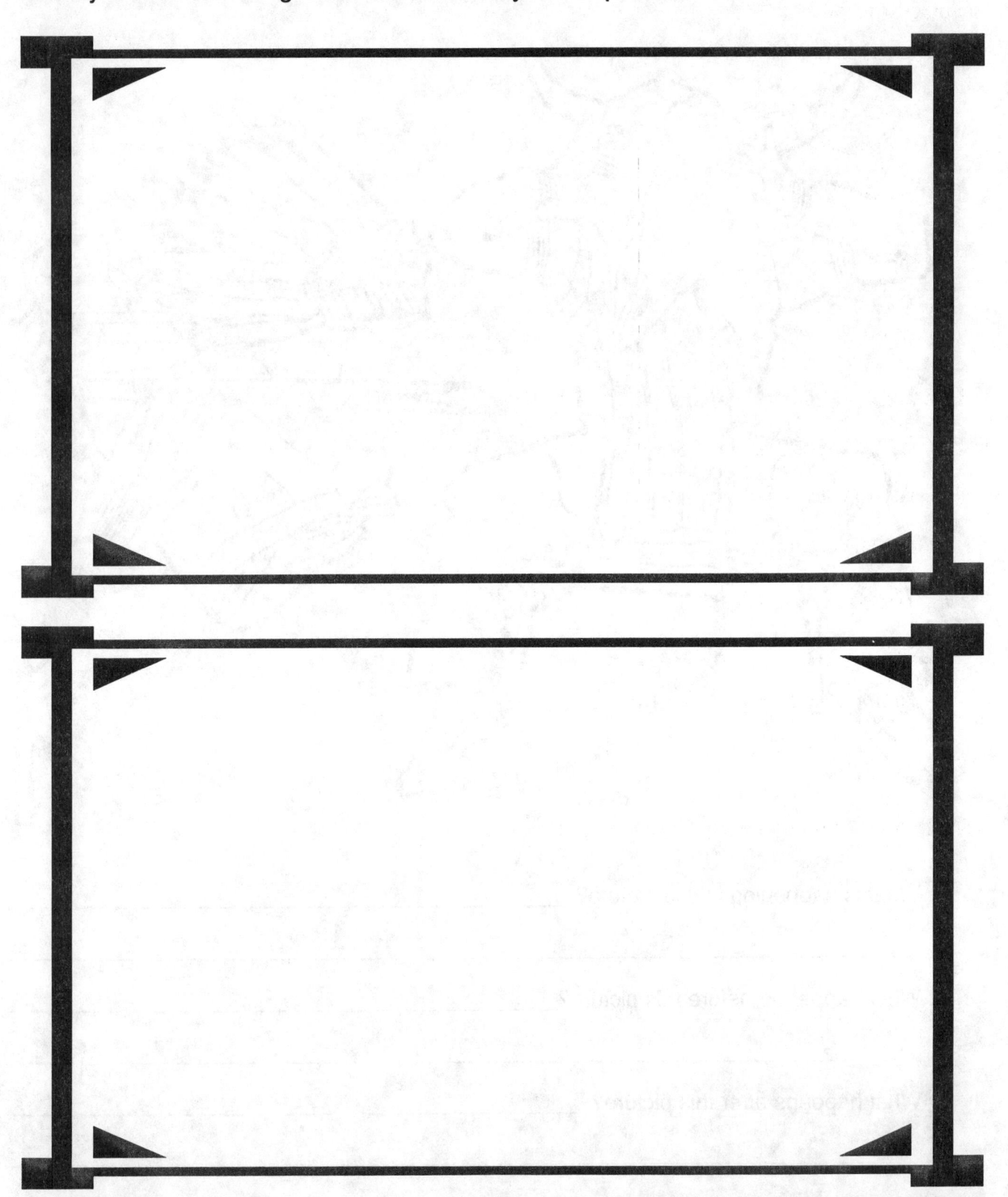

© Teacher Created Materials, Inc.   47   #476 Learning Through Literature—Native Americans

Plains

Name_____ Date _____

Reading a Picture

Look carefully at the picture and then answer the questions below it.

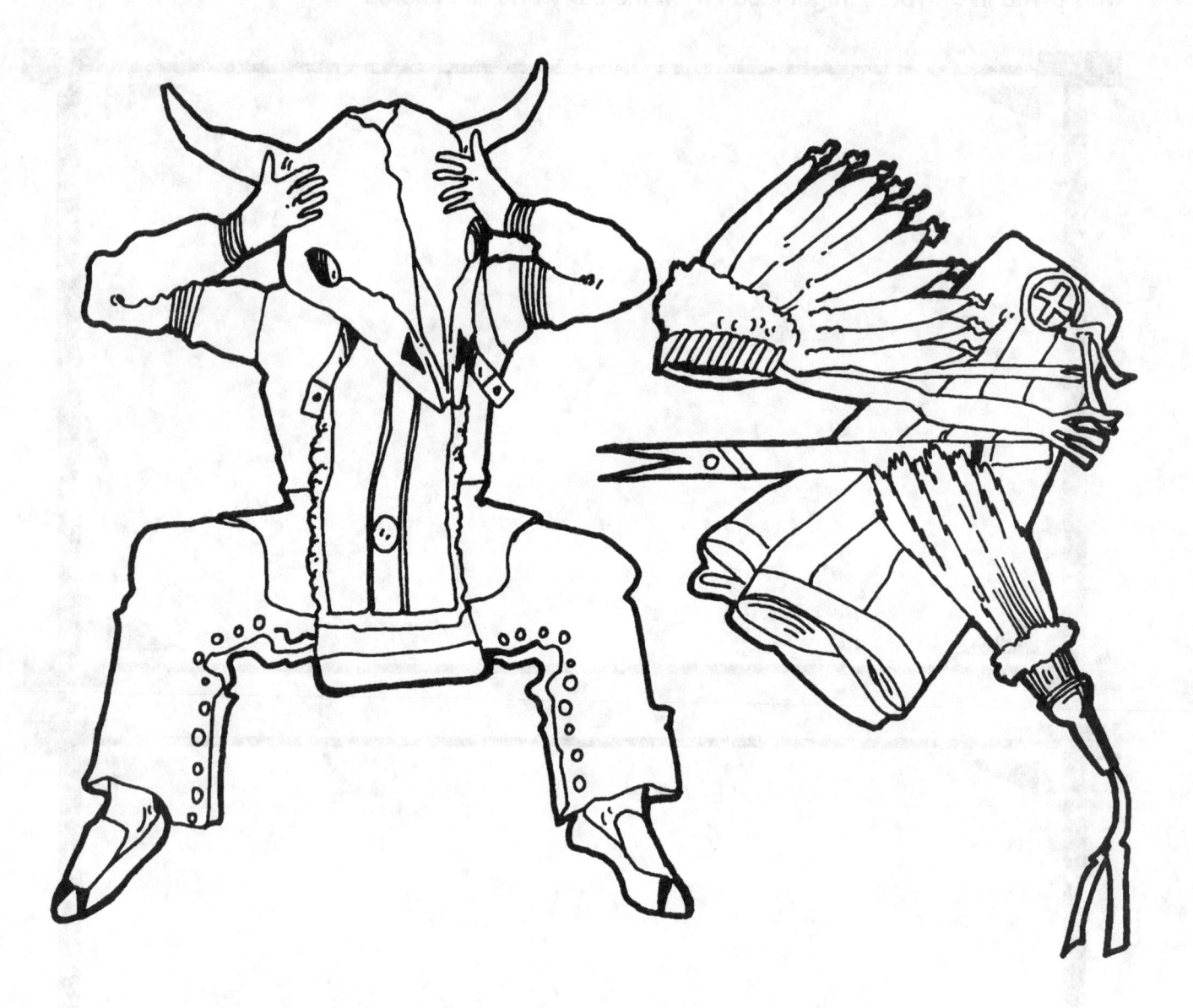

1. What is happening in this picture? _____
   _____

2. What happened before this picture?_____
   _____

3. What happens after this picture? _____
   _____

#476 Learning Through Literature—Native Americans

Plains

The Cheyenne

Author: Dennis B. Fradin

Publisher: Children's Press, 1988

Summary: This informational book provides a brief story of the Cheyenne Indians through interesting text and photographs of actual Cheyenne life.

Prereading Activity:

Read aloud the title of the book. Then ask the students to tell you what they think of and/or know about the Cheyenne and create a word web. For example:

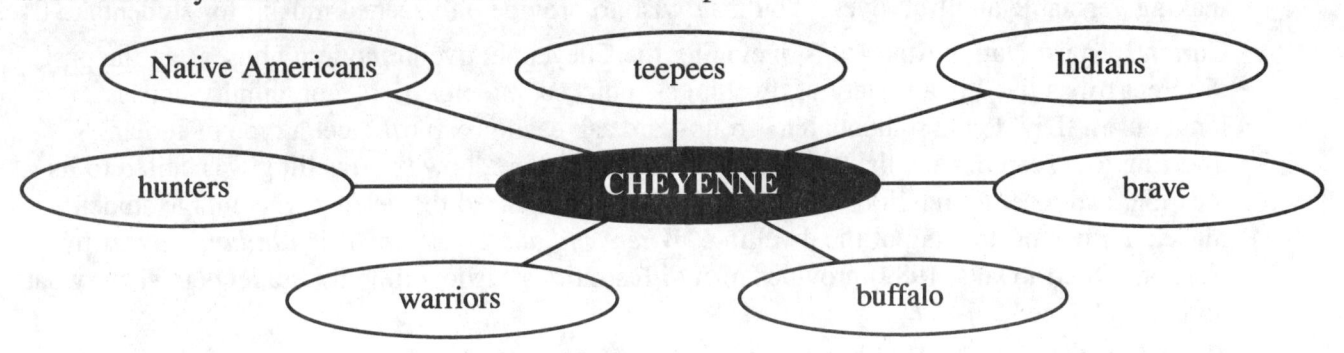

[Word web with CHEYENNE in center, connected to: Native Americans, teepees, Indians, hunters, brave, warriors, buffalo]

Key Words, Concepts, and People:

- reservation
- roaming
- Cheyenne
- lances
- counting coup
- Milky Way

Postreading Discussion Questions:

1. Where did most of the Cheyenne live? *(Answers may vary but could include the following: originally in the eastern United States and later in Oklahoma and Montana.)*

2. What tribes were the greatest enemies of the Cheyenne? *(They were the Kiowa, Crow, and Pawnee.)*

3. What was considered the bravest thing a Cheyenne warrior could do to an enemy? *(Count coup—touch him with a stick or other object.)* Why was this considered brave? *(Answers may vary.)*

4. The Cheyenne were not happy about the white settlers coming to America. Why? *(Answers may vary but could include that they took their land and killed all the buffalo.)*

5. What was Custer's Last Stand? *(It was a famous battle in which the Sioux and Cheyenne Indians joined together to fight the cavalry led by George Armstrong Custer.)*

6. Describe the life of a Cheyenne today. *(Answers may vary but could include the following: Many live on reservations; they maintain many of their customs and traditions; children are taught both their native language, and English.)*

© Teacher Created Materials, Inc.   49   #476 Learning Through Literature—Native Americans

Plains

The Cheyenne (cont.)

Learning Activities:

- **K-W-L (page 51)** Before reading, have students complete steps 1 and 2. After reading, have students complete step 3.
- *The Cheyenne* is one of many books in the "A New Time Book" series about Native Americans. Other books include *The Apache, The Cherokee, The Chippewa, The Choctaw, The Hopi, The Navajo, The Seminole,* and *The Sioux*. Gather several of these books and allow time for students to read about and compare and contrast the different tribes.
- Discuss how the Cheyenne lived very close to nature. They grew or hunted their own food, made their own clothes, and healed themselves with herbs and remedies. Many used fruits and vegetables to create decorative dyes. Tell students how fruits and vegetables become dyes: spinach can be boiled and the liquid can dye cloth green onion can be boiled for yellow dye; raspberries can be mashed for red dye. Provide an opportunity for students to experiment with making vegetable and fruit dyes. You may wish to provide unbleached muslin for students to dye.
- Currently, most Native Americans, including the Cheyenne, live in modern houses. In the past, different tribes lived in a variety of dwellings—chickee, pueblos, tipis, community houses, longhouses. Divide the students into groups and ask each group to select a type of Indian dwelling to research. Ask them to find out who lived there, how the dwelling was suited to its location, and whether religious and cultural beliefs influenced the design. Encourage students to make a replica or drawing of the dwelling. *Where Indians Live: American Indian Houses* by Nashone (Sierra Oaks, 1989) provides many illustrations. Allow time for students to share what they have learned.
- **Word Cards (page 52)** Divide students into small groups. Distribute a set of the word cards to each group. Ask students to assemble the cards into categories according to their own knowledge of those words or their predictions of how those words might be used in *The Cheyenne*. Allow the groups to share their various categories and to provide a rationale for the placement of the word cards within specific groups. Have each group record the categories and the words in each. After reading *The Cheyenne,* have students sort the word cards into new categories, if necessary, based on information gleaned from the text. Again, allow time for sharing the reasons for placement of the words into specific categories.
- **Diamonte Poem (page 53)** On the chalkboard, show the form and rules for a diamonte poem. Have students complete the activity sheet to write a diamontic poem about the Cheyenne. Allow time for students to share their poems.

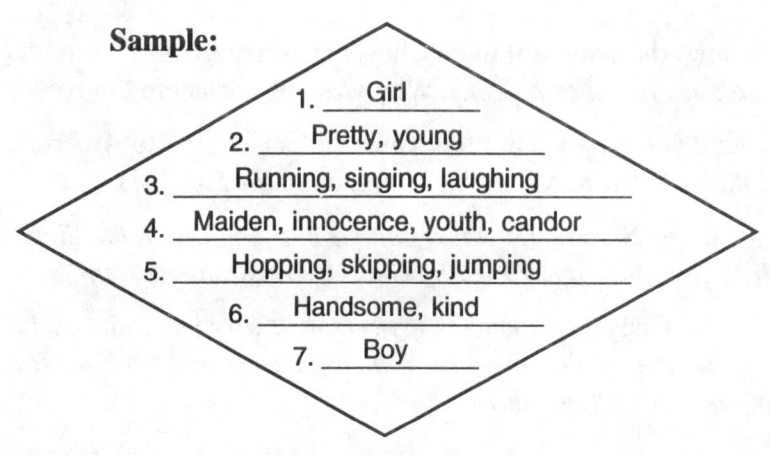

Sample:

1. Girl
2. Pretty, young
3. Running, singing, laughing
4. Maiden, innocence, youth, candor
5. Hopping, skipping, jumping
6. Handsome, kind
7. Boy

Plains

Name_____ Date_____

K-W-L

Complete steps 1 and 2 before you read *The Cheyenne*. Complete step 3 after you have read the story.

1. K— What **I** know about the Cheyenne.

2. W— What **I** want to find out about the Cheyenne.

3. L— What **I** learned and still need to learn about the Cheyenne.

Plains

Word Cards

reservation	hunting
lances	bows
arrows	wars
teepees	settlers
earth lodges	fishing
farming	buffalo
antelope	horses
spirits	elk
roaming	festivals

Plains

Name _____ Date _____

Diamonte Poem

A diamonte poem is written in the shape of a diamond. Follow the guidelines below and create a diamonte about Cheyenne people.

Line 1: one word *(a noun or pronoun)*
Line 2: two words *(adjectives describing line 1)*
Line 3: three words *("-ing" verbs showing action related to line 1)*
Line 4: four words *(nouns, the first two relating to line 1, the last two to line 7)*
Line 5: three words *("-ing" verbs showing action related to line 7)*
Line 6: two words *(adjectives describing line 7)*
Line 7: one word *(a noun or pronoun, often the opposite of the word in line 1)*

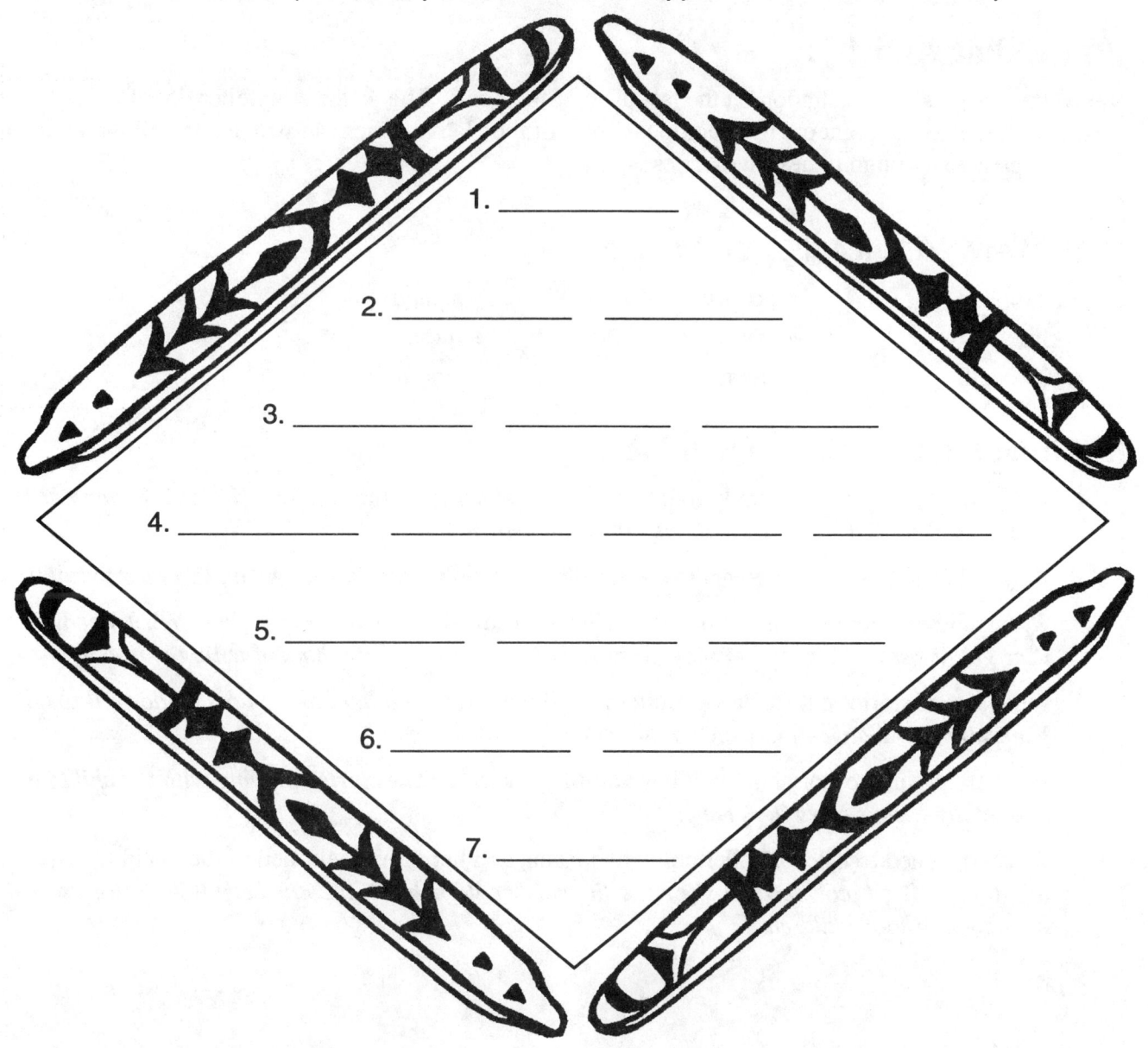

1. _____

2. _____ _____

3. _____ _____ _____

4. _____ _____ _____ _____

5. _____ _____ _____

6. _____ _____

7. _____

© Teacher Created Materials, Inc. #476 *Learning Through Literature—Native Americans*

Southwest

The Storyteller

Author: Joan Weisman

Illustrator: David P. Bradley

Publisher: Rizzoli International Publications, 1993

Summary: *The Storyteller*, a clay figure made by the Cochiti Pueblo people, plays an important role in this story about the developing friendship between a young Native American girl displaced from her pueblo and an old woman who lives in the same housing project. The illustrations are by a Native American artist.

Prereading Activity:

Show the students the illustration on the last page of the book. This is the storyteller doll that is featured in the book. Point out the traditional dress of the Native American woman and all the children who are gathered around to hear her stories.

Key Words, Concepts, and People:

- pueblo
- kiva
- Kokopelli
- pottery
- ancestors
- stoop
- sipapu
- mesa
- storyteller

Postreading Discussion Questions:

1. Why were Rama and her family living in the city, away from the pueblo? *(Rama's father was ill and in the hospital. They were in the city to be near him while he got well.)*

2. Why did Miss Lottie want Rama to come up to visit her? *(She was lonely and wanted to talk.)*

3. When neither Rama nor Miss Lottie knew what to say, Rama had a bright idea. What was it? *(She got her storyteller doll to show to Miss Lottie. It made them think of telling stories.)*

4. What sort of stories did Rama's grandfather tell her? *(He told her stories handed down through generations of Native American storytellers.)*

5. What effect did the storyteller doll have on Miss Lottie? *(She started playing with the children and telling them stories from her life.)*

6. What happened to the storyteller doll when Rama and her family returned to the pueblo? *(Rama left it with Miss Lottie because she knew the doll would help Miss Lottie keep telling stories to the neighborhood children.)*

Southwest

The Storyteller (cont.)

Learning Activities:

- Native Americans from the Cochiti Pueblo, as well as many other Native Americans, have a long tradition of storytelling. These stories are handed down from generation to generation. Have students bring written permission from their parents that it is okay for them to tell a story that everyone in their family knows and tells. Ask volunteers to share their families' stories.

- **Pueblo Storyteller Doll (page 56)** The Pueblo storyteller doll is often made of pottery by Native Americans from the Cochiti Pueblo. Have students complete the activity sheet. Ask partners to read their stories to each other.

- **Pueblo Daily Life (page 57)** At the Cochiti Pueblo, Rama had many things to do. Discuss with children the things they do each day. Have them complete the activity sheet and display the sheets on a bulletin board.

- Tell the students that people from the Cochiti Pueblo are part of the Anasazi culture. Ask children to look in the encyclopedia and other books from the library and classroom to find out several facts about the Anasazi culture. Ask children to report these facts to the class as a whole and then make a list of things about the Anasazi culture. Put this list on the bulletin board and have students draw pictures to illustrate the items on it.

- People from the pueblo culture are excellent potters and basket makers. The work of pueblo potters and basket weavers is highly prized and sought after as collected objects. Ask students to find pictures of pottery and baskets in *The Storyteller*. Also have students do library research to find other pictures of pueblo works. Give students an opportunity to draw pictures of the baskets and pots and hang the drawings around the room.

- **Pueblo Dwellings (page 58)** A pueblo is where a large group of Anasazi settled. These settlements are more than 800 years old. Discuss with students some reasons the Anasazi would have chosen the places they did for their pueblos.

- **Chaco Canyon (page 59)** Tell the students that Chaco Canyon, located in northern New Mexico, is a remarkable example of Anasazi culture. Have volunteers read aloud the facts on the activity sheet. Allow time for students to answer the questions, and then discuss the answers as a class. **Answers:** 1. 10 miles 2. 300, 3. They used animals and people power. 4. They needed a steady supply of water to grow crops and to serve the needs of a large population. 5. Mexico.

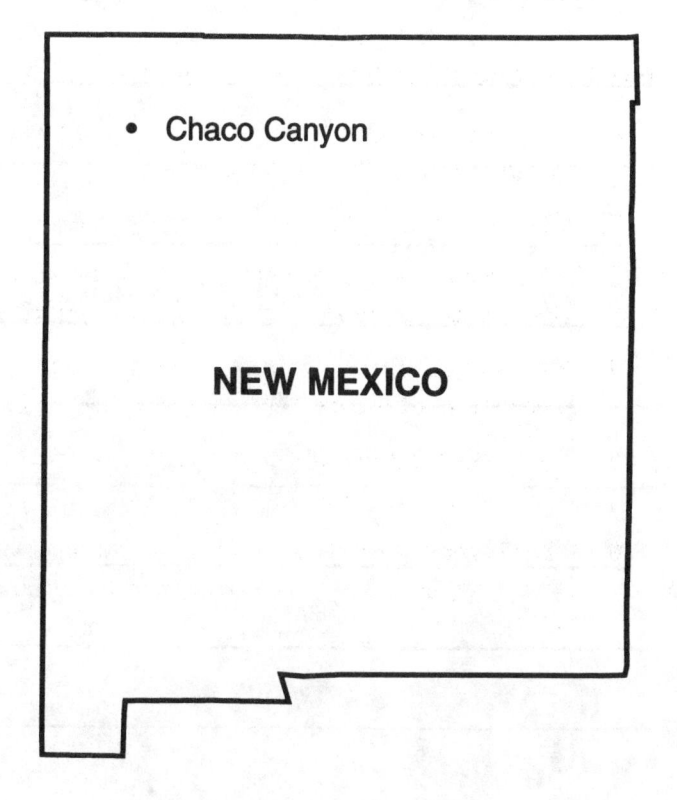

- Chaco Canyon

NEW MEXICO

© Teacher Created Materials, Inc. 55 #476 Learning Through Literature—Native Americans

Southwest

Name _____   Date _____

Pueblo Storyteller Doll

The Native Americans from the Cochiti Pueblo tell stories in public and to their children. Write a story that you think they might tell. Remember that some of the stories that were told by Native Americans of the Cochiti Pueblo address tales about coyote the trickster, corn maidens, and their ancestors.

_____
_____
_____
_____
_____
_____
_____
_____

#476 Learning Through Literature—Native Americans   56   © Teacher Created Materials, Inc.

Name _____ Date _____

Southwest

Pueblo Daily Life

Rama had hundreds of things to do when she lived at the Cochiti Pueblo. In the first column, list things that Rama did. In the second column, list similar things that you do. One is done for you.

Rama	Me
1. *Watch the women make pottery.*	*Watch mom sew.*
2.	
3.	
4.	
5.	
6.	
7.	
8.	

© Teacher Created Materials, Inc.   #476 Learning Through Literature—Native Americans

Southwest

Name _____ Date _____

Pueblo Dwellings

Below are descriptions of how and where Native Americans settled in their pueblos. In the box next to each of these descriptions, write why you think the Native Americans chose as they did. The first one is done for you.

Pueblo Settlement	Why
Pueblos were settled on high cliffs.	for protection from invaders
Pueblos were settled near water.	
Pueblos were settled near trading routes.	
Pueblos were settled near fertile land.	
They settled where they would have adequate rainfall.	
They settled where there was a supply of wood.	
They settled where they would have dirt that had a high clay content.	

#476 Learning Through Literature—Native Americans 58 © Teacher Created Materials, Inc.

Southwest

Name _____ Date _____

Chaco Canyon

Read the facts about Chaco Canyon and then answer the questions that follow.

- Chaco Canyon was settled between A.D. 900 and A.D. 1200.
- The canyon was 10 miles long.
- There were 8 major pueblos located in the canyon.
- Over 200,000 logs were used to build the pueblos.
- Nearly 400 miles of roads linked the pueblos.
- As many as 5,000 people lived in the pueblos.
- Canals were used to create a sophisticated irrigation system.
- Turquoise was imported from Mexico.

1. How long is Chaco Canyon?

   _____

   _____

2. During how many years was the Chaco Canyon settled?

   _____

   _____

3. How did the Anasazi get the logs to the canyons?

   _____

   _____

4. Why did they develop such a sophisticated irrigation and canal system?

   _____

   _____

5. Where did the Anasazi get their turquoise?

   _____

   _____

© Teacher Created Materials, Inc.   59   #476 Learning Through Literature—Native Americans

Southwest

Aztec, Inca, and Maya

Author: Elizabeth Baquedano

Illustrator: Photographs by Michel Zabe

Publisher: Alfred A. Knopf, 1993

Summary: This book gives a comprehensive picture of the MesoAmerican and Andean people and their cultures. The topics covered include history, survival techniques, domestic customs, religious beliefs, and artistic expression.

Prereading Activity:

Elicit from students their thoughts about what Native Americans are and where they lived. Discuss the Native American cultures that flourished in the Americas—North America (including Mexico), Central America, and South America.

Key Words, Concepts, and People:

- Pre-Columbian
- MesoAmerica
- Andes
- Aztecs
- Inca
- Maya
- pyramid
- civilizations
- sacrifice
- glyphs
- Quetzalcoatl
- gold

Postreading Discussion Questions:

1. Where were the two main areas that supported these civilizations? *(The two main areas were MesoAmerica, which included much of Mexico and Latin America where the Aztecs and Maya lived, and the Andes Mountains on the west coast of South America, where the Inca lived.)*

2. Did these civilizations build cities? Explain. *(Yes. In MesoAmerica large cities dominated by pyramids and temples were built. In the Incan Empire incredible stone walls were built as part of forts and cities such as Cuzco and Michu Picchu.)*

3. Could these people write? *(The Incas left no written records, but in MesoAmerica there was an extensive system, based on glyphs, that recorded their history and ceremonies.)*

4. What religion did they have? *(They worshiped many gods, mostly those connected to natural forces or aspects of nature and particularly the sun. They built impressive temples to these gods and practiced human sacrifice to keep them happy.)*

5. What art forms did they have? *(These Native Americans were great artists, creating monumental sculpture, intricate textiles, infinitely varied clay pottery and sculpture, and extensive works in gold.)*

6. What happened to these civilizations? *(They were destroyed in the 16th century by Spanish Conquistadors—Cortes in Mexico and Pisarro in Peru. However, descendants of these original people still inhabit MesoAmerica and the Andean regions.)*

Aztec, Inca, and Maya *(cont.)*

Learni...

...e Americas in the 16th century, the Aztec, Maya, and Inca people ...ny years and had created great civilizations. Have students draw a ...South America and with different colors show the areas that ...s: Aztec, Maya, and Inca.

... students that the pottery was an important part of the ...ever, pottery was not often used for decoration but was more ... sheet and allow time for students to share their answers.

...tions were very important to the MesoAmerican lifestyle. These ...of a child; weddings; deaths; and coming of age, particularly for

...s an important part of the MesoAmerican and Inca life. The large ...rate and beautiful. Have students identify the different names we

...cuss with the class the concept of sacrifice. Lead them into ... sacrifices and how they were used by the Indians. Allow ...gs about this practice. Assign the activity sheet.

...quipu was used for counting and keeping track of mathematical information. ...raw a picture of a quipu and to indicate through the length and color of the ... that represents a mathematical number. Tell the students to explain at the bottom ...what each length of string represents, what each color represents, and what each .... Show them the picture of the quipu on page 40 of the book to assist them in ...ir own.

...hat Peruvian men carried small bags over their shoulder that contained valuable ...them to identify what they think the Peruvian man carried in the bag. Ask them to ...ow it compares with what we carry in purses or wallets. Remind students that the ...merican people had valuable metals and stones similar to the ones that we value today. H... students identify what some of these precious metals and stones were and to briefly describe how they were used. Remind them that the most precious metal of all was gold.

- Divide students into small groups and have each group choose one of the following animals to investigate—armadillo, alpaca, ocelot, puma, jaguar, fox, and vicuña. Have each group provide the following information about its animal: where it lived in MesoAmerica, its influence on MesoAmerican life, the extent to which the animal still exists and is protected, and the role the animal plays now.

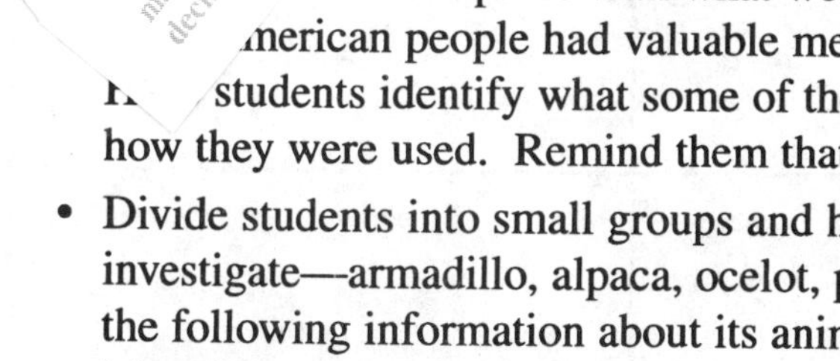

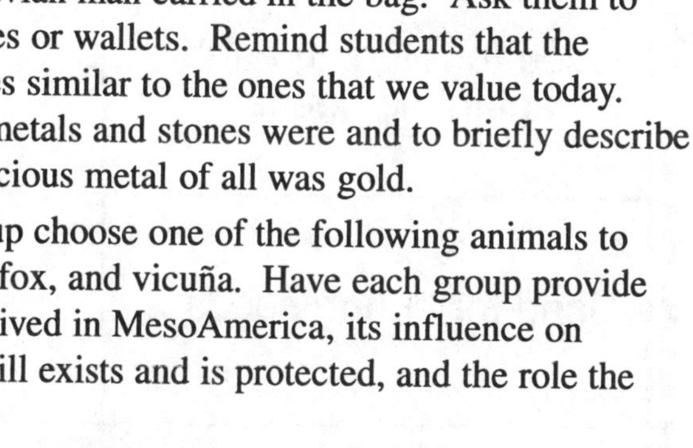

Southwest

Name _____ Date _____

Useful Pottery

The use of pottery in the MesoAmerican life is provided in the first column. In the second column is a space to describe what utensil we would use. In the third column is a space for you to draw a picture of what the MesoAmerican pottery piece would look like.

MesoAmerican Pottery	Modern Utensil	Pottery Piece
Used for grinding corn		
Used for carrying water		
Used for cooking		
Used for cutting meat		
Used for digging earth and planting seeds		
Used for curing seeds		
Used for holding fires		
Used for making beads		

Southwest

Name _____ Date _____

Celebration

The first column describes how MesoAmericans celebrated important events. In the second column, describe how your family celebrates the same events.

MesoAmericans	Your Family
Wedding	**Wedding**
When a couple was married, the man's cloak and the woman's blouse were tied together during the ceremony. Persons who attended brought something from their own homes to help the couple start their new life.	
Birth of a Child	**Birth of a Child**
Elaborate foods were prepared to celebrate the new life. The celebration lasted for several days.	
Death	**Death**
The dead were buried in underground tombs.	
Starting to School	**Starting to School**
Boys from noble families started their formal educations at age 15. The school was in a temple and run by priests.	

© Teacher Created Materials, Inc.   63   #476 Learning Through Literature—Native Americans

Southwest

Name _____ Date _____

Worship

At the top of each box, write the name of a god worshiped by the Incas and MesoAmericans. Under the god's name, describe why you think they worshiped the god. The first one is done for you. On the back of this activity sheet, draw a picture of one of the gods and label it.

Rain God

Rain was extremely important to grow crops for food.

Southwest

Name_____ Date_____

Human Sacrifice

Read the facts and then answer the questions.

- Human sacrifice was part of the Indian religious ritual.
- Priests performed the sacrifices.
- Their religion told them it was necessary to sacrifice to satisfy the gods.
- Sacrifices took place during important festivals.
- Most sacrifices took place in high places such as mountaintops.
- Men, women, and children were sacrificed, as were animals.
- The human heart was the most important gift the people could offer the gods.
- The arms and legs of the sacrificed person were often eaten by the people who were there at the sacrifice.

1. Why do you think the heart was considered the most important offering to the gods?
   _____

2. Why do you think the Indians believed it was important to make human sacrifices instead of just animal sacrifices?
   _____

3. During what times of the year do you think most sacrifices were likely to occur?
   _____

4. What is the word we use to describe a human being eating another human being?
   _____

5. How do you think the Indians chose the person to be sacrificed?
   _____

6. How do you feel about the practice of human sacrifice? About animal sacrifice?
   _____
   _____
   _____
   _____

© Teacher Created Materials, Inc.　　　65　　　#476 Learning Through Literature—Native Americans

Southwest

Arrow to the Sun

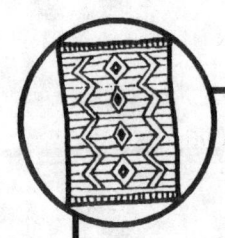

Author: Gerald McDermott

Illustrator: Gerald McDermott

Publisher: The Viking Press, 1974

Summary: This beautifully illustrated book recounts an ancient pueblo story about a boy who searches for his heritage by undergoing a series of trials before he returns to his people.

Prereading Activity:

Show the children the designs inside the cover of the book. Ask them whether they have ever seen any such designs before. Elicit descriptions of Native American designs they may be familiar with through traveling or from movies. Have students offer their ideas about what the cloud symbol reminds them of. Brainstorm with students possible reasons why all the illustrations in this book are stylized.

Key Words, Concepts, and People:

- pueblo
- spirit
- arrow maker
- ceremony
- corn planter
- Lord of the Sun
- kiva
- pot maker
- chambers

Postreading Discussion Questions:

1. Why do you think the Native Americans in this book felt the sun was so important? *(They realized that the sun provides the warmth and light the world needs and thought that it must be a great power.)*

2. Why was only the arrow maker and not the corn planter or the pot maker able to help the boy? *(Answers may vary but could include that the boy needed to be sent to the sun, and the arrow maker could shoot him there like an arrow.)*

3. What were the four chambers of ceremony that the boy needed to pass through? *(They were the Kiva of Lions, the Kiva of Serpents, the Kiva of Bees, and the Kiva of Lightning.)*

4. Does the illustration of the Lord of the Sun remind you of anything you have seen from the pueblos? *(Answers may vary but could include that it resembles some kachina dolls.)*

5. Look at the illustrations of each of the passages the boy makes through the kivas. Have students tell what happens in each. *(Answers may vary but could include that he tames the lions, he makes the serpents into hoops, he gets the bees to make honeycombs, and the lightning transforms him so that he has the power of the sun.)*

6. How did the people celebrate his return to the pueblo? *(They celebrated with the Dance of Life.)* What other things do you think they might celebrate by dancing? *(Answers may vary.)*

Southwest

Arrow to the Sun (cont.)

Learning Activities:

- Explain to students that Pueblo Indians lived in sophisticated communities of connected homes much like modern condominiums. Pueblos were built on hilltops and on the steep sides of mountains for protection. Show the class several pictures of the pueblos in the book. Provide art supplies and have students make their own pueblo.

- Obtain records or tapes of Pueblo Indian chants from the library and play them in class.

- Explain to students that the kiva is a sacred religious place located in or near the pueblo and that some pueblos have more than one kiva. Kivas are similar to churches, but they are underground and only men can go in them. Ask students to generate a list of the kinds of things that were done in the kiva and the kinds of decisions that were made there.

- Tell students that one of the ways in which the Pueblo Indians represent stories of their culture is through kachina dolls. Find a book on kachina dolls and show the pictures to the class. Have students draw their own kachina dolls and display the drawings in the classroom.

- **Snake Dance (page 68)** The Hopi, like other pueblo people, honor animals. The Hopi feel that snakes are an indication of rain which was important to their survival because it was needed to grow crops for food. Assign the activity sheet. **Answers:** 1. To keep the snake from hurting the dancer, 2. Answers may vary, 3. So that the snakes would go and tell the god of water to bring rain, 4. Answers may vary.

- **Make a Spirit Doll (page 69)** Remind students that kachina dolls are spirit figures and that their dolls should represent things that are personally meaningful to them. Assign the activity sheet; then, provide supplies with which students can make spirit dolls.

- **Scrambled Words (page 70)** Assign the activity sheet to complete in class. Go over the students' papers in class; then have each student write a sentence that relates to the picture of the bow and arrow. Remind them to scramble one word in the sentence. Have pairs trade papers, unscramble the word in his/her partner's sentence, and read it aloud to the partner. **Answers:** 1. kiva 2. pottery 3. sun 4. pueblos 5. mesa 6. corn 7. father

Southwest

Name _____ Date _____

Snake Dance

Read the following story about the snake dance and then answer the questions that follow.

> Did you know that the Hopi people felt that snakes would help bring rain for their crops? Most of us are afraid of even seeing a snake, much less catching one. However, Hopi men went into the woods and forests and looked for snakes. They looked for snakes by checking under bushes and rocks. They found as many snakes as they could for the snake dance. Sometimes they found rattlesnakes and other poisonous snakes. When the men caught a snake, they sprinkled it with cornmeal that had been pressed by the shaman, and then they put the snake in a bag. When they got ready for the ceremony of the snake dance, the shaman took the snakes to the center of a circle of men. As each man danced by the shaman, he gave him a snake to put between his teeth. Another dancer stood nearby with a feather and swatted at the snake to keep it from harming the dancer who was holding it between his teeth. At the end of the ceremony, the snakes were taken back to the edge of the mesa and released in all directions so that they could go ask the god of water to bring rain.

1. Why did a man with a feather stand near the snake dancer?

    _____

2. Would you want to be a snake dancer? If you were a young Hopi boy, do you think you would feel differently?

    _____

3. Why did the Hopi people let the snakes go in all directions?

    _____

4. Would you like to be the shaman or a dancer during the snake dance? Why?

    _____

5. Draw a picture of a snake dancer on the back of this activity sheet.

#476 Learning Through Literature—Native Americans   68   © Teacher Created Materials, Inc.

Southwest

Name_____ Date _____

Make a Spirit Doll

Follow the directions to make your own spirit doll. Be sure to name it and to describe its special powers.

Materials Needed:

- An empty tube from toilet paper or paper towels
- Cotton balls
- Cloth
- Construction paper
- Rubber band
- Glue
- Scissors
- Materials to decorate the doll, such as pasta, buttons, yarn, ribbon, cotton balls, leaves, feathers, small rocks, and twigs

Directions:

1. Cut a square of fabric about 4" x 4" (10 cm x 10 cm).
2. To make the head, put several cotton balls in the center of the fabric square, pull the fabric up around the cotton balls, and secure them inside with a rubber band.
3. Place the head on one end of the tube and glue the fabric tails to the tube.
4. Using more cloth or construction paper, glue a skirt to the doll.
5. For arms, poke twigs or rolled construction paper into the tube and glue them on.
6. Decorate your doll.

Name of Spirit Doll: _____

Special Powers of Spirit Doll: _____

Draw a picture of your spirit doll on the back of this activity sheet.

© Teacher Created Materials, Inc.　　　69　　　#476 *Learning Through Literature—Native Americans*

Southwest

Name _____ Date _____

Scrambled Words

Unscramble the boldfaced words to complete each sentence about Pueblo Indian life.

1. The sacred place where the Pueblo Indians go is referred to as a **viak**. _____

2. The Pueblo Indians used clay from the earth to make **roptye**. _____

3. According to the book, the boy was brought to earth by an arrow that came from the **nus**. _____

4. The Native American people who live in **epluosb** are known by the same name as these cliff dwelling homes. _____

5. A high area of ground with a flat surface and steep sides is referred to as a **esma**. _____

6. A very important crop to the pueblo people is **norc**. _____

7. The boy went to look for his **hertaf** because the other boys were making fun of him. _____

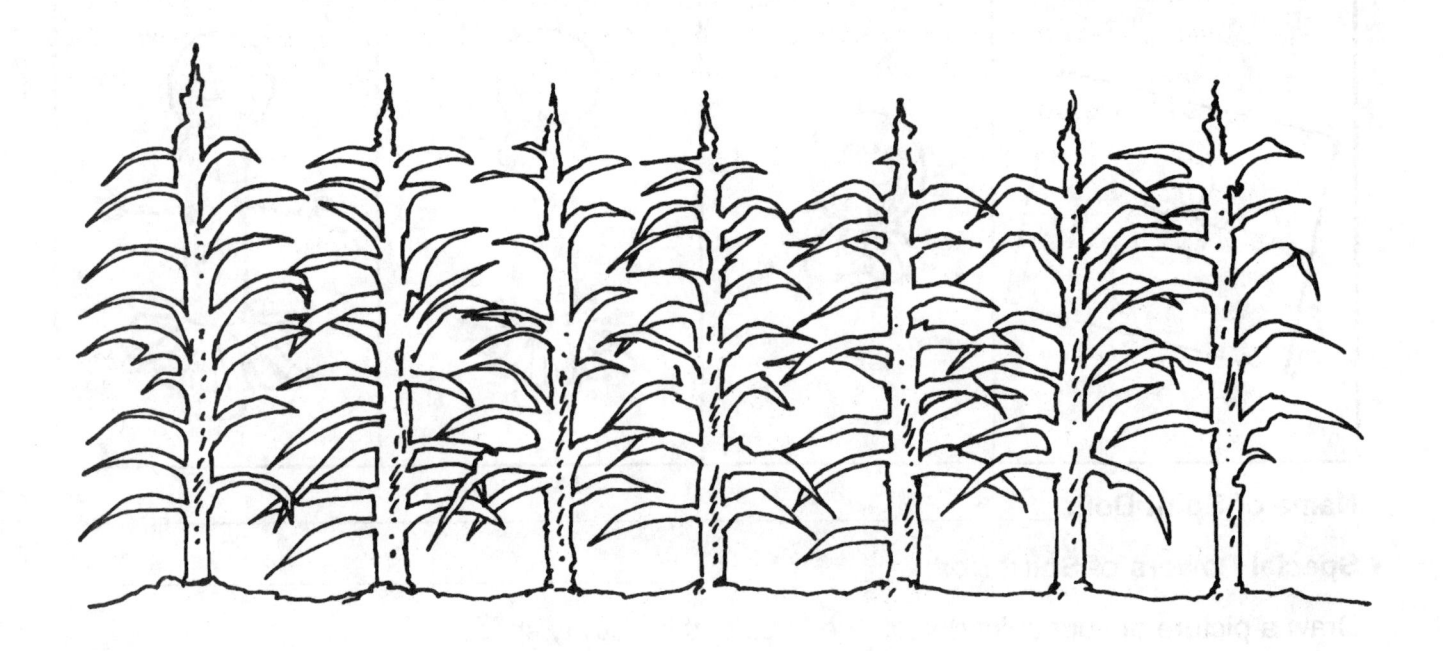

#476 Learning Through Literature—Native Americans 70 © Teacher Created Materials, Inc.

Southwest

The Hopi

Author: Ann Heinrichs Tomchek

Publisher: Children's Press, 1992

Summary: This book presents the history, background, and culture of the Hopi (hope-ee) Indians of the American Southwest. The Hopi are an ancient, colorful, and peaceful people.

Prereading Activities:

Show students the pictures of the kachina dolls on page 31 of this book. Discuss with the class what they think the dolls might be used for besides toys. Explain to students that the dolls are used in the religious ceremonies of the Hopi people.

Key Words, Concepts, and People:

- mesa
- Anasazi
- pueblo
- Seven Cities of Cibola
- revolt
- traditionals or progressives
- sipapu
- kiva
- kachina

Postreading Discussion Questions:

1. What is the origin of the Hopi? *(No one knows for sure. They seem to have always been there. Their ancestors are called the Anasazi. Ancient sites of the Anasazi with ruined buildings, pottery, and other artifacts have been found in the area where the Hopi live.)*

2. Who were the first Europeans to meet the Hopi, and what were they looking for? *(An expedition led by the Spanish explorer Coronado was the first to meet the Hopi, in 1540. The Spanish had conquered Mexico and were looking farther north for the legendary Seven Cities of Cibola, which were supposed to be fabulously wealthy. What they found instead were the villages of the pueblo people like the Hopi.)*

3. According to Hopi belief, how did the first people come to the world? *(They climbed up through the original sipapu, which is deep in the Grand Canyon.)*

4. What are the Hopi pueblos like? *(They are villages of apartment-like buildings made of dried mud [adobe] and stone. Ladders that can be pulled up behind people are used to climb up to the upper stories.)*

5. What is the ceremonial room of the pueblo people? *(It is the kiva, which is a room dug into the ground that you enter by going down a ladder. It has a fire pit in the center and a small hole in one end as a reminder of the original sipapu. The Hopi and other pueblo people hold religious ceremonies in the kiva.)*

6. Tell about the kachinas. *(Kachinas are ancestor spirits that help the Hopi by bringing rain, helping the corn grow, and other good things. During religious ceremonies, dancers wear masks and paint themselves to resemble the kachinas. Kachina dolls are made to help the children learn about kachinas.)*

Southwest

The Hopi *(cont.)*

Learning Activities:

- Explain to students that the kiva is much like a church in terms of its religious significance. Religious and political decisions are made in the kiva. The way to enter the kiva is by ladder, because the kiva is built underground. On the walls of the kiva are drawings and paintings of sacred animals and spirits. Have students draw a picture of a kiva and decorate the inside walls.

- Show students the pictures of the kachina dolls on page 31 of the book. Check out a book from the library that shows bigger pictures of kachina dolls. Tell students that some names for the kachina dolls include Stone-Eater, Mudhead, Wolf, and Buffalo. Discuss with students how they think the dolls got these names. Have students draw a picture of a kachina doll and name it.

- **About the Hopi (page 73)** Assign the activity sheet to complete in class, and have volunteers read the items aloud. **Answers:** 1. customs, ritual, 2. mesas, 3. language, 4. ancestors, 5. grind, 6. traditional, 7. progressives, 8. reservation

- Discuss with students the Hopi belief that people came into the world from a hole, or sipapu, located in the Grand Canyon. Ask volunteers to tell how they believe people came into the world.

- Show the class the pictures of the pueblos on page 21 of the book. Ask them to identify several types of housing used by Native Americans. Ask students to identify how the lifestyles and cultures of the tribe would influence the kind of housing they used. For example, compare hunter/gatherers and farmers.

- Corn is the most important crop to Hopi Indians. Have students list on a separate sheet of paper ways in which the corn plant was used in Hopi culture.

- **Hopi Calendar (page 74)** Discuss with the class how special events occur during each year. Assign the activity sheet.

- The Hopi potters were excellent at using clay to make beautiful colored pots. Ask students to work in groups of two to three. Give each group a piece of clay. Show them how to roll the clay to make coil pots. Have each group design a pot. See illustration on this page.

- The flute provided traditional music for the Navaho and Hopi. See if the library will obtain some authentic Indian traditional music. Play it for the students. Obtain flutes and give the children the opportunity to play them.

- **Birds and Animals (page 75)** Tell the class that the Hopi felt close to and respected the birds and animals in their environment. Discuss whether non-Indians feel close to animals or birds and how their feelings may differ from those of the Hopi. Assign the activity sheet for students to take home and complete with a family member.

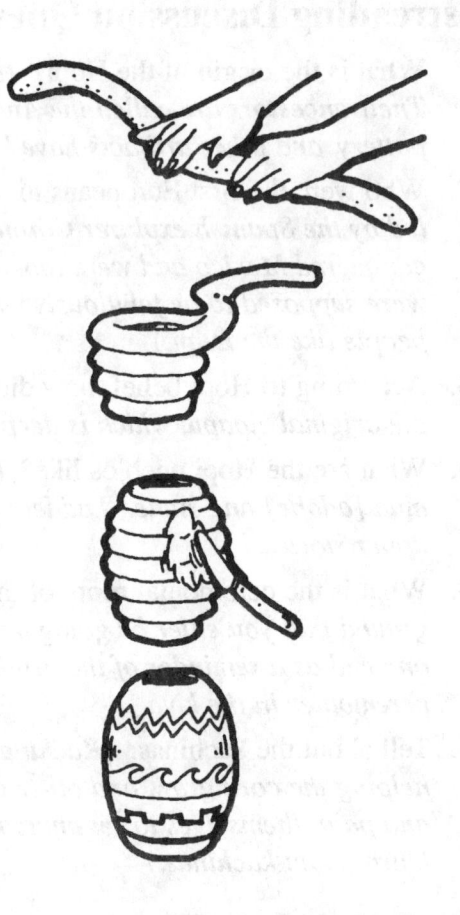

Southwest

Name _____ Date _____

About the Hopi

On the blanks, write the words from the box that best complete the sentences.

language	ancestors	mesas	canyon
progressives	grind	customs	pueblo
sacred	reservation	ritual	traditional

1. The _____ of the Hopi people are practices that they have carried on for a long time. For example, their sacred dances are part of their _____.

2. To help them stay safe from others, the Hopi people chose to live on high, flat land with steep sides, or _____.

3. The Hopi speak a _____ that is very different from that of the other Pueblo people.

4. The Hopi feel that their _____, or the people who came before them, provided guidelines about how they should live their lives.

5. Corn is a very important crop for the Hopi. They _____ the hard kernels in order to make cornmeal.

6. Some Hopi people are _____ and want to keep the Hopi way as it has always been.

7. Other Hopi are considered _____ because they want change and more contact with other people.

8. An area of land set aside for Native Americans to live on is a _____.

© Teacher Created Materials, Inc.   73   #476 Learning Through Literature—Native Americans

Southwest

Name _____ Date _____

Hopi Calendar

Read the special events in the Hopi calendar. Then, for each of the months provided, write in events that are special to your family during the year.

Hopi Calendar

January	February	March	April
Kachina Dances	Deer Ceremony	Announcement of the Coming of the Kachinas	Crop Dances

May	June	July	August
Crop Dances	Summer Solstice	Homecoming Ceremony	Flute Ceremony

September	October	November	December
Women's Fertility Dances	Women's Basket Dance		Winter Solstice

Southwest

Name _____ Date _____

Birds and Animals

Below are lists of birds and animals important to the Hopi. Write the names of some of the animals and birds that are found in your area. How do you think Native Americans would have used them in their lives? Get help from a family member to finish this page.

Birds and Animals Found in the Hopi Environment

Birds	Animals
eagle	buffalo
hawk	fox
crow	wolf
hummingbird	beaver
	bear

Birds and Animals Found in My Area

Birds	Animals

How would the birds and animals in your area have served as resources to the early Americans who lived there?

_____
_____
_____
_____
_____
_____
_____
_____

© Teacher Created Materials, Inc.   75   #476 Learning Through Literature—Native Americans

Southwest

Hawk, I'm Your Brother

Author: Byrd Baylor

Illustrator: Peter Parnall

Publisher: Aladdin Books, 1986

Summary: A contemporary Native American boy in the Southwest who has always wanted to fly steals a young hawk from its nest. He calls this hawk his brother and through his relationship with the bird, gains a feeling for flying.

Prereading Activity:

Ask the children if they have ever wished that they could fly. Ask whether any of them have seen a hawk or an eagle soaring. Have volunteers describe what they feel when they watch a bird in flight. Discuss the fact that some birds are sacred to many Native American tribes.

Key Words, Concepts, and People:

- hawk
- brother to brother
- canyon
- magic people
- offering
- bird's spirit

Postreading Discussion Questions:

1. Near the beginning of the book, there is an illustration of Rudy dreaming. In this dream, he sees the head of a hawk. Look at the hawk's eye. What is it? Turn the picture sideways. What do you see? *(The eye is the head of a Native American. The top of its head is his upraised arm, and he holds something that helps form the mouth. The hawk is largely formed by the Native American.)*

2. From looking at the illustrations, how can we tell what part of the country Rudy Soto lives in? *(We can tell by the vegetation in general, but the tall cacti with arms, the saguaros, grow in only one region of the Southwest—southern Arizona.)*

3. When reading the story, did you feel that Rudy would ever actually fly like the hawk? *(Answers may vary.)*

4. Can hawks be tamed? *(Yes, they can. In the Middle Ages in Europe, hawks and falcons were trained to fly on command, hunt small birds and animals for their masters, and return to their master's arm. It was considered a sport and was called falconry.)*

5. Did Rudy or the hawk change more? *(Answers may vary, but Rudy definitely understood more about flying through his experiences with the hawk.)*

6. Do you think Rudy did the right thing when he let the hawk go? Why or why not? *(Answers may vary.)*

7. What do you think the title of the book means? *(Rudy and Hawk got to be "brothers" as they learned more about each other.)*

Southwest

Hawk, I'm Your Brother *(cont.)*

Learning Activities:

- Rudy Soto wanted very much to be a bird so he could fly. Ask students what animal they would most like to be. Have them draw pictures of the animals and describe what they would do if they were the animals.

- This story is about a boy who fell in love with the way birds fly. Have student groups research how many types of hawks there are and write a report about one kind to present orally to the class.

- Discuss with students the Native American custom of changing a boy's name during his lifetime. First, his parents name him for something he likes to do for example, Runs Fast. When a boy comes of age (around 15), a shaman gives him his permanent name. Have students think about the boy in this story, Rudy Soto. Elicit from the class examples of the name his parents might have given him. Then have students give examples of names the shaman may have given him.

- **Rudy and the Hawk (page 78)** Assign the activity sheet in which students finish and illustrate a story about Rudy and the hawk. Allow time to share story endings and drawings in class.

- **Problem Solving with Rudy (page 79)** Assign the activity sheet to complete in class. Have volunteers read aloud the problems and give the answers. Then have student volunteers read their own questions aloud and let the class solve them. **Answers:** 1. 60 times, 2. 104 times, 3. 3 hours, 4. 7 birds (including the hawk that is his friend)

- **Conversation with Rudy (page 80)** Have students imagine talking with Rudy about flying. Elicit from students their feelings about flying. Assign the activity sheet.

- Go bird watching. Take the class to an area of the school grounds where there are usually birds or take a field trip for bird watching. Have students draw pictures of and describe the birds they see. When you return to the classroom, have students research in bird books to determine the kinds of birds they saw.

- Make a bulletin board display entitled "Birds We've Seen." Have groups of students work together to draw and color pictures of the birds, write descriptions of their appearances, and indicate what they eat.

Southwest

Name _____ Date _____

Rudy and the Hawk

Read the incomplete story below and then write an ending for it. Illustrate your story.

Rudy had not seen his hawk friend for several days. He tried again and again to call him with a hawk call. Still the hawk did not come. Worried, Rudy climbed to the mountaintop near where the hawk was born and where he had first found him.

_____
_____
_____
_____
_____
_____
_____
_____
_____
_____
_____
_____
_____
_____
_____
_____
_____
_____

Southwest

Name _____ Date _____

Problem Solving with Rudy

Read and answer the problems below. Then write two of your own problems and the answers. Be ready to share your work with the class.

1. When Rudy freed the hawk, it jumped up and down 20 times in one minute. It continued to jump for three minutes. If it jumped at the same speed for all three minutes, how many times did the hawk jump up and down?

2. Rudy dreamed about flying. In his dreams, he soared over valleys and mountaintops. He dreamed of flying at least two times a week every week of the year. How many times a year did he dream of flying?

3. Rudy saw his friend the hawk flying across the valley toward the forest 90 miles away. If the hawk was flying 30 miles per hour, how long would it take it to get to the forest?

4. Rudy climbed to the top of a mountain to see his friend the hawk. On his way up, he saw three birds. When he got to the top, he saw an eagle. Then, as he waved to his friend the hawk, he saw two other hawks. How many birds did Rudy see in all?

5. _____

6. _____

© Teacher Created Materials, Inc. 79 #476 Learning Through Literature—Native Americans

Southwest

Name _____   Date _____

Conversation with Rudy

Complete the blanks in the following conversation between you and Rudy. Use the information from the story to guide your answers.

Rudy: "The thing I want to do more than anything else in the world is _____

_____."

Me: "What I want to do most is _____

_____."

Rudy: "If I could fly, I would soar over the valley and dip down into the woods and _____

_____."

Me: "If I could fly, I would _____

_____."

Rudy: "It would be so much fun to fly because _____

_____."

Me: "It would be great fun to fly because _____

_____."

Rudy: "The bird I would fly like is the _____

_____."

Me: "I would fly like _____

_____."

Southwest

Big Thunder Magic

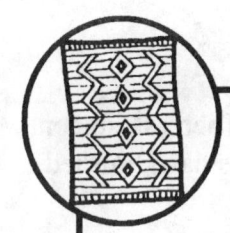

Author: Craig Kee Strete

Publisher: Greenwillow Books, 1990

Summary: Nanabee, a sheep, lives with the Great Chief in a pueblo. A small, timid ghost named Thunderspirit sleeps next to Nanabee. One day the Great Chief and Nanabee go to the city, and Thunderspirit follows them. While in a park, Nanabee is captured and taken to a zoo. Thunderspirit uses his magical powers to rescue Nanabee.

Prereading Activity:

Show students the cover of the book and read aloud the title. Tell the class that this is book about a small ghost with magical powers. Ask them what people or characters they know or have read about that have magical powers. Discuss with the class the belief in magical powers and whether any of them have such powers.

Key Words, Concepts, and People:

- pueblo
- medicine
- magic
- ghost
- desert
- lightning
- thunder
- chief

Postreading Discussion Questions:

1. Describe where Nanabee and Thunderspirit live. *(Answers may vary.)*

2. Do you think the Great Chief knew about Thunderspirit? Why or why not? *(Answers may vary.)*

3. Do you think Nanabee knew about Thunderspirit and could see him? Why or why not? *(Answers may vary.)*

4. Was it a good idea for the Great Chief to take Nanabee with him to the city? Why or why not? *(Answers may vary.)*

5. Why did Thunderspirit like to sleep next to Nanabee? *(Answers may vary.)*

6. Why do you think the Great Chief went to the city? *(Answers may vary.)*

7. Do you think the Great Chief knew that Nanabee was taken to the zoo? Why or why not? *(Answers may vary.)*

8. What do you think would have happened to Nanabee if Thunderspirit hadn't performed his magic to get him out of the zoo? *(Answers may vary.)*

Southwest

Big Thunder Magic (cont.)

Learning Activities:

- **Magic for Me (page 83)** Discuss with the class Thunderspirit's magical acts. Then ask students to imagine they have a magic sheep and assign the activity sheet. When students have finished, allow time for sharing wishes.

- **Word Jumble (page 84)** Assign the activity sheet in which students unscramble words from the story. Answer aloud in class. **Answers:** 1. desert, 2. pueblo, 3. thunder, 4. magic, 5. ghost, 6. chief, 7. lightning, 8. medicine

- **Magical Character (page 85)** Challenge students to imagine they are authors who will write books about magical characters. Assign the activity sheet. Allow time for students to share their magical characters. Select one of these magical characters and as a class, write a short story about the character.

- Discuss with students the events in the story that could actually happen and those that could not. On the chalkboard, write "make-believe" at the top of one column and "real" at the top of another column. As you talk about the various events in the book, have students tell you which column the events belong in and why. Write the events in the appropriate column.

- In this story, Thunderspirit and Nanabee lived in a pueblo. Obtain a copy of *Where Indians Live: American Indian Houses* by Nashone (Sierra Oaks Publishing Co., 1989). Show the class the variety of homes in which Indians lived and discuss the advantages and disadvantages of each. Allow students to look through the book on their free time.

- *The Pueblo* by Charlotte and David Yue (Houghton Mifflin, 1986) is a good reference that provides excellent illustrations and information about the Pueblo Indian homes. Allow time for the children to look through the book. Then discuss what Thunderspirit's and Nanabee's lives were like living in a pueblo.

- Discuss with children why Nanabee could not stay in the hotel with Great Chief. Divide students into pairs or small groups and ask them to list other places where Great Chief may want to go that Nanabee would not be allowed to go. Ask them to also think about and list places in the city that Great Chief might have taken Nanabee instead of the park.

#476 Learning Through Literature—Native Americans © Teacher Created Materials, Inc.

Southwest

Name _____ Date _____

Magic for Me

Pretend that you have a magic sheep friend like Thunderspirit. On the sheep below, write the magic you would like him to do for you.

© Teacher Created Materials, Inc. 83 #476 Learning Through Literature—Native Americans

Southwest

Name _____ Date _____

Word Jumble

Unscramble each word below and write it on the line next to the scrambled word. On the line under each word, write a sentence using the word.

1. seterd _____

   _____

2. blopeu _____

   _____

3. ruhndet _____

   _____

4. acmig _____

   _____

5. gotsh _____

   _____

6. fiche _____

   _____

7. gnihlintg _____

   _____

8. nemedici _____

   _____

Southwest

Name_____ Date_____

Magical Character

Thunderspirit created magic out of his medicine bag. Imagine that you are writing your own book about a magical character. Answer the questions below.

1. Thunderspirit was a ghost. What would your character be? _____
   _____

2. What would you name the character? _____

3. What would your character need to make magic? _____
   _____

4. Where would your character live? _____

5. Who would come to your character for magic? Why? _____
   _____

6. Describe the magic that your character could do. _____
   _____

Draw your magical character.

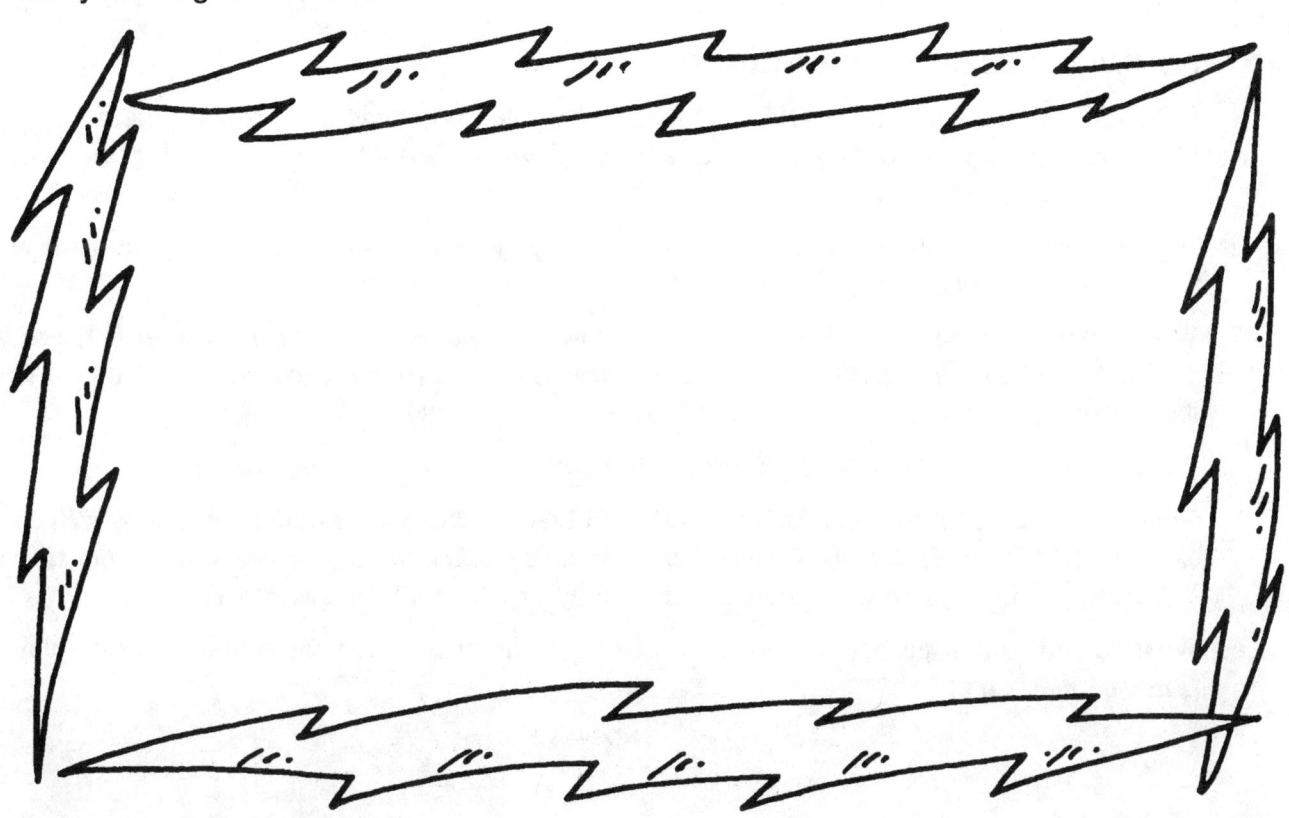

© Teacher Created Materials, Inc. 85 #476 Learning Through Literature—Native Americans

Southwest

Annie and the Old One

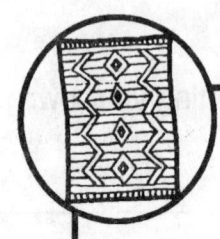

Author: Miska Miles

Illustrator: Peter Parnell

Publisher: Little, Brown & Co., 1971

Summary: Annie, a young girl, comes to accept the impending death of her grandmother as she recognizes the wonder of life.

Prereading Activity:

This is a story about the fun Annie and her grandmother had together. Annie's grandmother always seemed to have time for her; Annie could not imagine life without her. Ask students if there is anyone they feel this way about. Who and why? How would they feel if they found out that person was dying?

Key Words, Concepts, and People:

- coyote
- weave
- mesa
- warp
- desert
- Navajo
- hogan
- loom

Postreading Discussion Questions:

1. What did the grandmother (the Old One) mean when she said would go to Mother Earth? *(Answers may vary but could include that she was going to die.)* How do you think grandmother knew she was going to die? *(Answers may vary.)*

2. How is Annie's life different from yours? *(Answers may vary.)* How is Annie's life the same as yours? *(Answers may vary.)*

3. What are some of the things Annie did to slow down her mother's weaving? *(She misbehaved in school, turned the sheep loose, and pulled the threads of yarn from the woven rug.)* How do you think Annie felt about doing these things? *(Answers may vary.)*

4. Would you like to be Annie's neighbor? Why or why not? *(Answers may vary.)*

5. Grandmother asked Annie and Annie's mother and father what they would like of hers. What did each one take? *(Annie took the weaving stick; Annie's mother, the rug; Annie's father, the silver belt.)* Do you think these were good choices? Why or why not? *(Answers may vary.)*

6. What do you think happened to the Old One (the grandmother) at the end of the story? Explain. *(Answers may vary.)*

Southwest

Annie and the Old One (cont.)

Learning Activities:

- **What Is It? (page 88)** Play some "I'm thinking of . . ." riddles with the class. Assign the activity sheet. Allow time for the class to read aloud their riddles and elicit answers from classmates. **Answers:** pueblos, Navajos, coyote, mesa, loom, warp, weave, desert
- **I Learned How (page 89)** Discuss with the class things they have learned to do, such as crafts, skills, or hobbies. Assign the activity sheet. Display students' activity sheets on a bulletin board entitled "Things We've Learned to Do."
- **Different Homes (page 90)** Discuss the differences in the types of dwellings in which people around the world live. For example, some people live in apartments, mobile homes, single family homes, cabins, and tents. Assign the activity sheet.
- Provide clay, sticks, bark, cardboard, glue, and yarn. Then ask the children to work in groups to make a replica of Annie's hogan.
- Annie liked to listen to stories her grandmother told. Ask students to invite their grandparents to come in and tell some of their stories to the class.
- Have students make colorful weavings. With a paper cutter, cut lengthwise a large number of one-inch strips (2.5 cm) from a lot of different colors of construction paper. Provide full sheets of construction paper, scissors, and glue or tape. Then have students follow these steps:
    1. Fold one piece of construction paper in half lengthwise.
    2. Along the fold line, cut slits one inch apart, leaving a one-inch border, and creating a "loom." (Caution students not to cut through the unfolded edge of the paper.)
    3. Open the paper loom and weave colored strips through it.

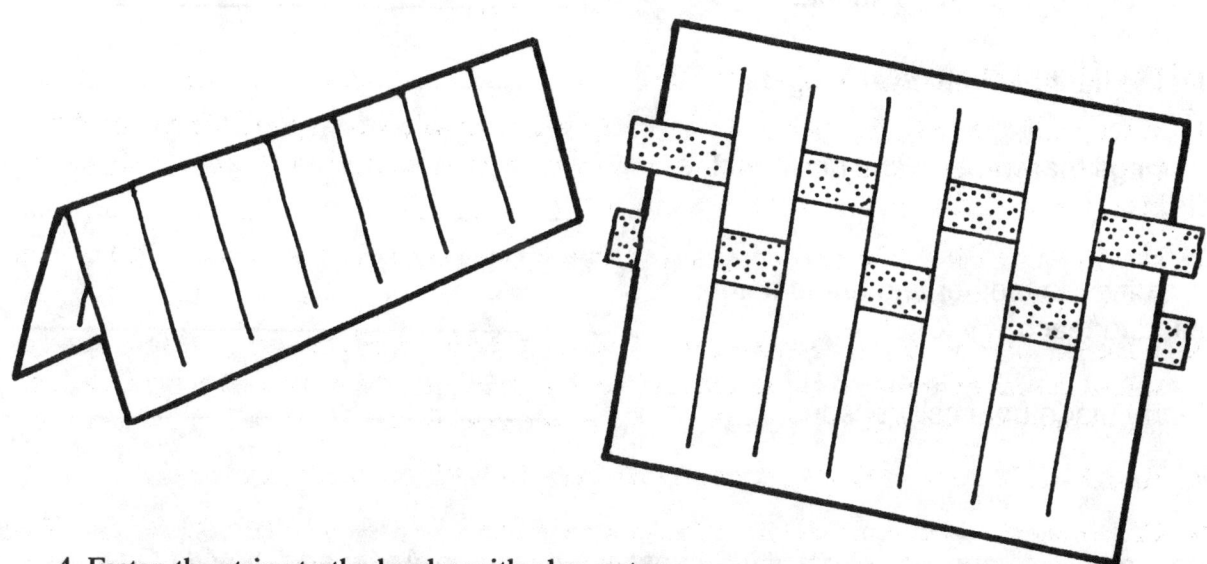

    4. Fasten the strips to the border with glue or tape.
- The fourth Friday in September is American Indian Day. Many states and/or communities celebrate this day. To help students learn more about Indian culture, write to Canyon Records, 4143 North 16th Street, Phoenix, AZ 85016, and ask for a catalog of records, cassettes, posters, slides, and other materials that relate to Native Americans. Have the class plan an American Indian Day celebration for their room.

Southwest

Name _____ Date _____

What Is It?

Use the words in the box to answer the questions below.

```
coyote        weaving       mesa          warp
desert        Navajo        pueblos       loom
```

I'm thinking of . . .   **What is it?**

what the Indians call their homes.   _____

the name of an Indian tribe.   _____

an animal that guards the Navajo hogans.   _____

the flat land near Annie's hogan.   _____

what the mother did her weaving on.   _____

the strings that went up and down on the
loom.   _____

something the mother and grandmother
wanted to teach Annie.   _____

dry land made up mostly of sand.   _____

Create some of your own "What is it?" questions based on *Annie and the Old One*. Share them with the class.

Southwest

Name_____Date_____

I Learned How

In the story *Annie and the Old One,* Annie learned how to weave. Think of something you have learned to do. Respond to the phrases below.

What I learned:_____

How I learned to do it: _____

When I learned to do it: _____

Draw a picture of what you learned to do.

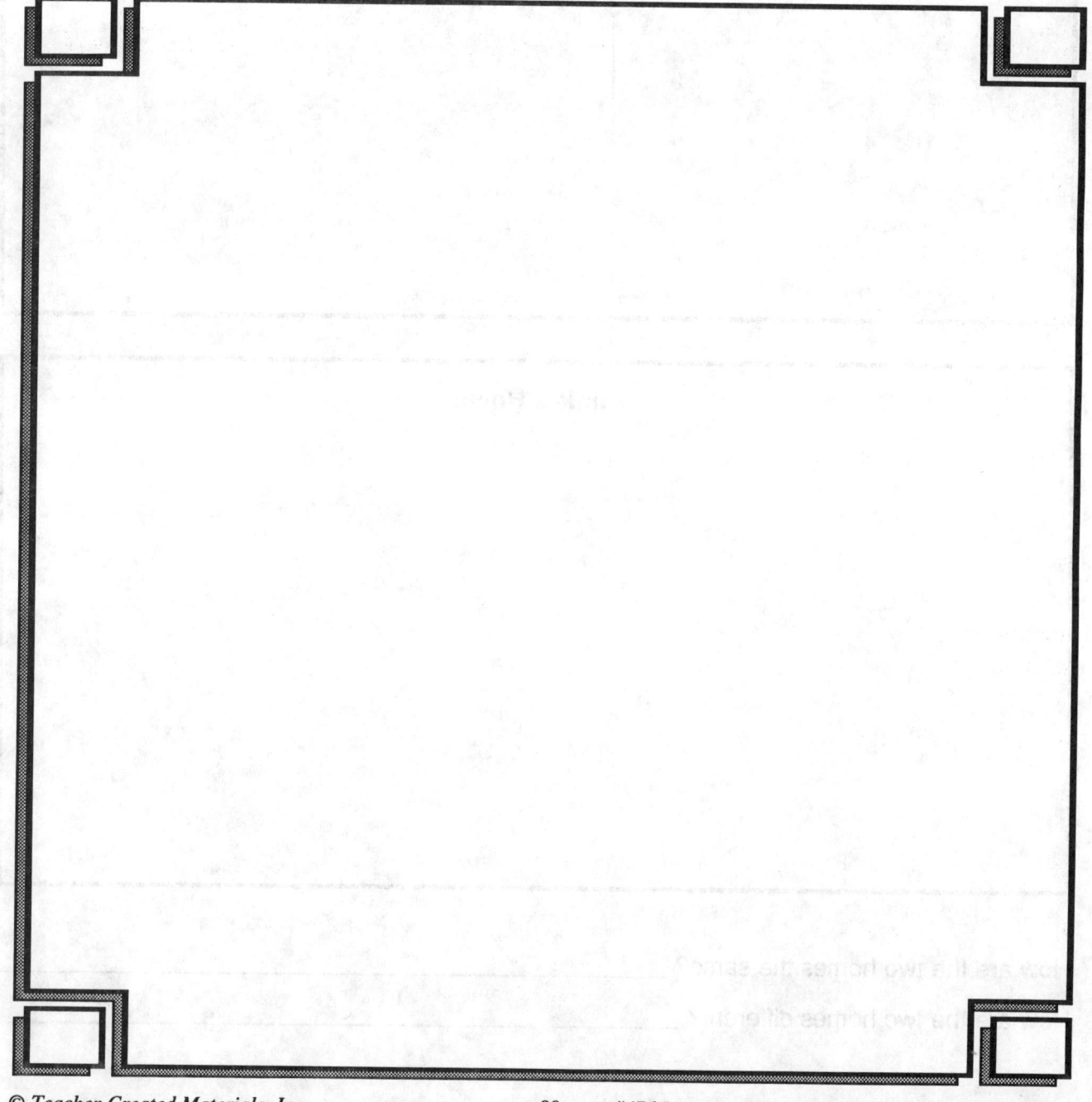

Southwest

Name _____ Date _____

Different Homes

In the first box, draw a picture of where you live. In the second box, draw a picture of where Annie lived.

My Home

Annie's Home

How are the two homes the same? _____

How are the two homes different? _____

Southwest

The Legend of the Indian Paintbrush

Author: Tomie dePaola

Illustrator: Tomie dePaola

Publisher: Putnam, 1988

Summary: This story explains how the Indian paintbrush got its name from a plant that grows on hills and in meadows in Texas and Wyoming. It has brightly colored spikes that bloom in the spring.

Prereading Activity:

In this story, a young Indian boy has a dream-vision that reveals that he will someday be a painter. Ask students if they have ever dreamed about what they will be when they grow up. Have students pretend they have dream-visions and draw pictures of what those visions were. Create a bulletin board from their pictures.

Key Words, Concepts, and People:

- tepee
- tribe
- vision
- fade
- warrior
- struggle
- custom
- deed

Postreading Discussion Questions:

1. Do you remember your dreams? What are some dreams you have had? *(Answers may vary.)*

2. Do you think dreams really mean anything to your "awake" life? *(Answers may vary.)*

3. Do artists today use the same kinds of art supplies as Little Gopher? How are they alike? How are they different? *(Answers may vary.)*

4. What was bothering Little Gopher? *(Answers may vary but could include that he was smaller than the rest of the children and could not keep up with them.)*

5. What did Little Gopher like to do when he was young? *(He liked to make toy warriors from scraps of leather and pieces of wood and decorate smooth stones with the red juices from berries.)*

6. How is Little Gopher's way of living different from yours? *(Answers may vary.)*

7. Why did Little Gopher finally get the colors he needed? *(He was faithful to the people and true to his gift.)*

Southwest

The Legend of the Indian Paintbrush (cont.)

Learning Activities:

- **Feather Words (page 93)** To review words from the story, assign the activity sheet to complete in class. Pair students and have them take turns showing a feather and having their partner pronounce the word on it. Give each student an envelope in which to keep his/her feathers.

- **When I Grow Up (page 94)** Discuss with the class that where they work will probably depend on what they choose to do for work. Assign the activity sheet and allow time for sharing.

- **My Legend (page 95)** Discuss with the class that a legend is a story handed down from the past that may seem believable but cannot be proven. Assign the activity sheet to complete in class and create a "Legends" bulletin board.

- Summarize and discuss with students the Author's Note at the end of the book, pointing out that the Indian paintbrush is the state flower of Wyoming. Elicit from students what the state flower of your state is. Then show a state flower or a picture of the state flower. Have students draw, color, and label pictures of their state flowers.

- **Fact or Opinion (page 96)** Discuss the difference between fact and opinion as described on page 96. Ask the students to complete the activity sheet, and then have them discuss their answers and sentences with each other in small groups.
  Answers: 1. F 2. O 3. F 4. F 5. F 6. F 7. F 8. O 9. F 10. F

- This author also wrote *The Legend of the Bluebonnet*. Read the story aloud to the class. Discuss how the legends of the flowers are alike and how they are different. Discuss with the class which story they liked better and why.

- At the end of this story, Little Gopher's name was changed to He-Who-Brought-the-Sunset-to-the-Earth. Have students list their family members' names on a sheet of paper. Challenge each student to think of a new name for each member of his/her family. Have them base the new name on something important or unique about the person. Allow time for students to share their names and explain why they chose them.

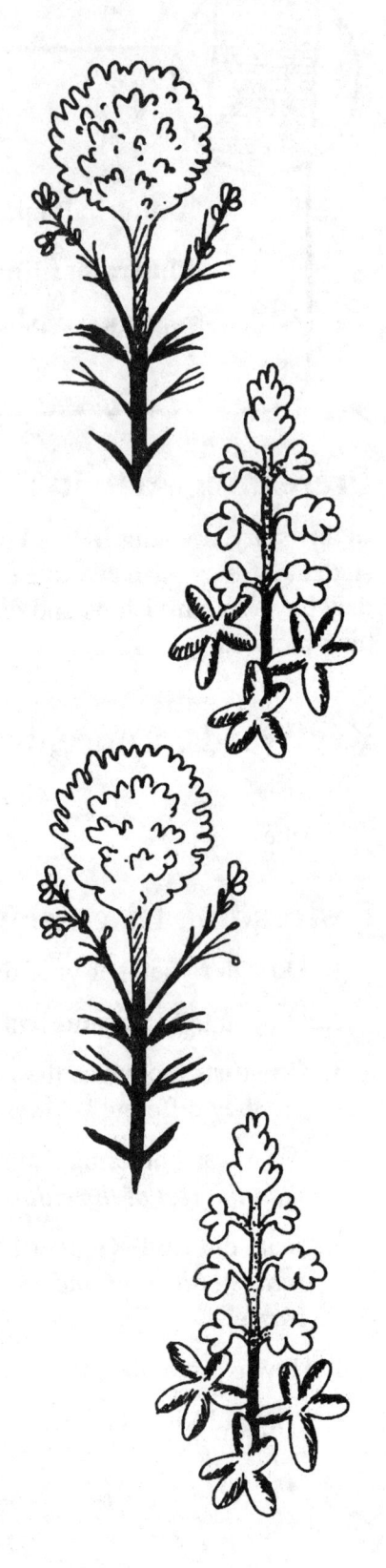

Southwest

Name _____ Date _____

Feather Words

Color the feathers, cut them out, and use them as sight cues as you pronounce the word on the feather to a partner.

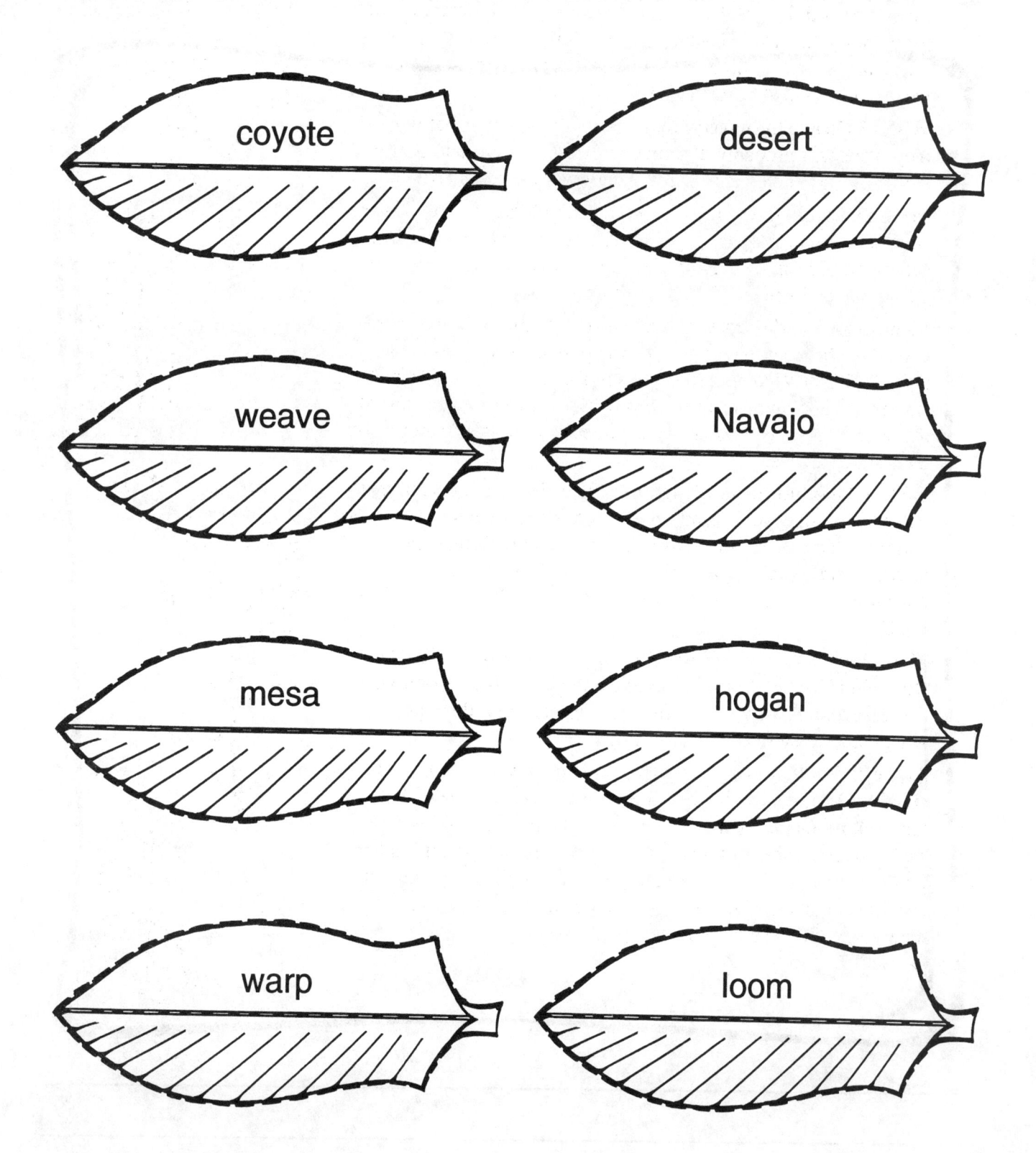

coyote

desert

weave

Navajo

mesa

hogan

warp

loom

Southwest

Name _____ Date _____

When I Grow Up

Draw a picture of you doing what you want to do and where you want to do it when you grow up. Then write below a sentence describing what you drew.

_____

#476 Learning Through Literature—Native Americans

Southwest

Name _____ Date _____

My Legend

Choose one of the questions below and create a legend to answer it. In the box, draw a picture of your legend and label the illustration.

1. Why does the sun come up in the east and set in the west?

2. Why are there four seasons?

3. Why do we have mountains?

4. Why are there stars in the sky at night?

5. Why are the oceans so big and deep?

The Legend of _____

Southwest

Name _____ Date _____

Fact or Opinion

A fact is something that can be proven to be true. An opinion is something that cannot be proven to be true. Read each sentence below. Put an **F** in the blank if the statement is a fact. Write an **O** in the blank if the statement is an opinion.

_____ 1. Little Gopher made brushes from the hairs of different animals.

_____ 2. Little Gopher was a good painter.

_____ 3. Little Gopher painted on the skins of animals.

_____ 4. His paints were made out of crushed berries, flowers, and rocks of different colors.

_____ 5. Little Gopher's mother and father worried about him.

_____ 6. Little Gopher had enough brushes to paint his pictures.

_____ 7. The other boys in the tribe were always riding, running, shooting their bows, and wrestling.

_____ 8. Everyone liked Little Gopher's paintings.

_____ 9. Little Gopher found the colors of the sunset.

_____ 10. At the end of the story, Little Gopher was called "He-Who-Brought-the-Sunset-to-the-Earth."

Write a sentence that states a fact. _____

_____

Write a sentence that states an opinion. _____

_____

#476 Learning Through Literature—Native Americans   96   © Teacher Created Materials, Inc.

Southwest

Knots on a Counting Rope

Authors: Bill Martin, Jr. and John Archambault

Illustrator: Ted Rand

Publisher: Henry Holt and Co., Inc., 1987

Summary: In this beautifully illustrated book, a young boy and his grandfather reminisce about the boy's birth and his exciting horse race.

Prereading Activity:

Discuss with the class the different story elements that constitute good literature: characterization, setting, theme, plot, and point of view. On the chalkboard, create a story web using these elements. For example:

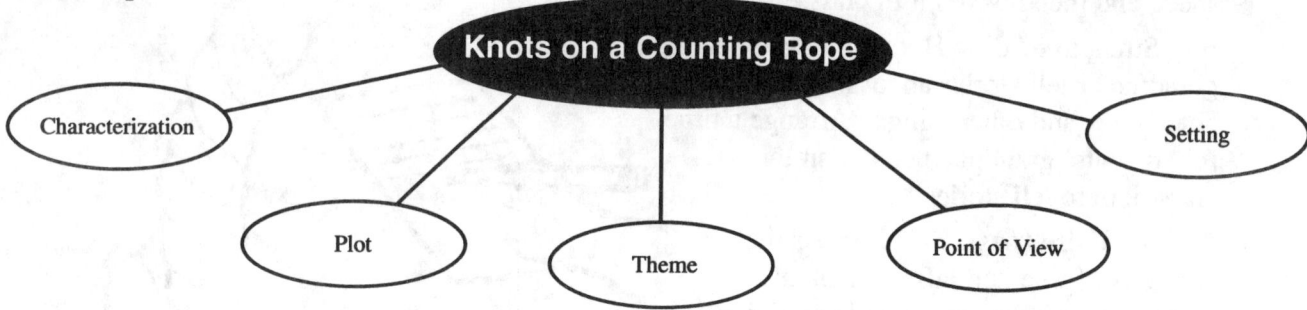

Knots on a Counting Rope — Characterization, Plot, Theme, Point of View, Setting

Then tell students to think about these elements as you read the story. Tell them you will add to the story web after reading *Knots on a Counting Rope*.

Key Words, Concepts, and People:

- hogan
- bobcat
- naming ceremony
- colt
- canyon
- frail
- foal
- galloping

Postreading Discussion Questions:

1. Where does this story take place? *(Answers may vary.)*
2. What was wrong with the little boy when he was born? *(Answers may vary but could include that he was sick, frail, and had vision problems.)*
3. Do you think this story is true or make-believe? *(Answers may vary.)*
4. What did Grandfather mean when he talked about the boy crossing dark mountains? *(Answers may vary but could include challenges the boy would face because of not being able to see.)*
5. Would you tell a friend to read this book? Why or why not? *(Answers may vary.)*
6. How might the boy's life have been different if he had not had his grandfather? *(Answers may vary.)*
7. Do you have someone you care for like the boy did his grandfather? Explain. *(Answers may vary.)*

Southwest

Knots on a Counting Rope (cont.)

Learning Activities:

- Give each student a piece of string about 36 inches (.9 m) long. Ask them to select one activity to keep track of, such as reading a book, completing homework, or learning spelling words. Have them tie a knot in their "counting rope" each time they complete their activity. At the end of a week, have each student show his/her counting rope, tell what the chosen activity was, and say how many times he/she completed it.

- **Make a Venn Diagram (page 99)** Brainstorm with students ways they are similar to and different from another class. Introduce the concept of a Venn diagram to show similarities and differences. Assign the activity sheet.

- **Sequence of Events (page 100)** Discuss sequencing with the class. Allow time for students to complete the activity sheet, and then discuss it in class.

- Boy Strength of Blue Horses enjoyed hearing his grandfather tell stories about how he was born, the horse race, and other things. Arrange a time for students' grandparents to visit the classroom to tell stories.

- **True or False (page 101)** Discuss the concepts of true and false. Then talk about how simple codes are devised, i.e., assigning a letter to correspond with a number. Assign the activity sheet. Have students raise their hands when they are finished. **Answers:** 1. T (A); 2. F (I); 3. T (N); 4. T (R); 5. T (W); 6. F (O); 7. F (B). Have the class as a whole give you the answer to the code word: RAINBOW.

- After reading the story, add to the word web you started in the Prereading Activity.

Southwest

Name _____ Date _____

Make a Venn Diagram

Write words or phrases about the the other class in one part of the circle, about your class in another part of the circle, and about both of the classes in the center part of circles.

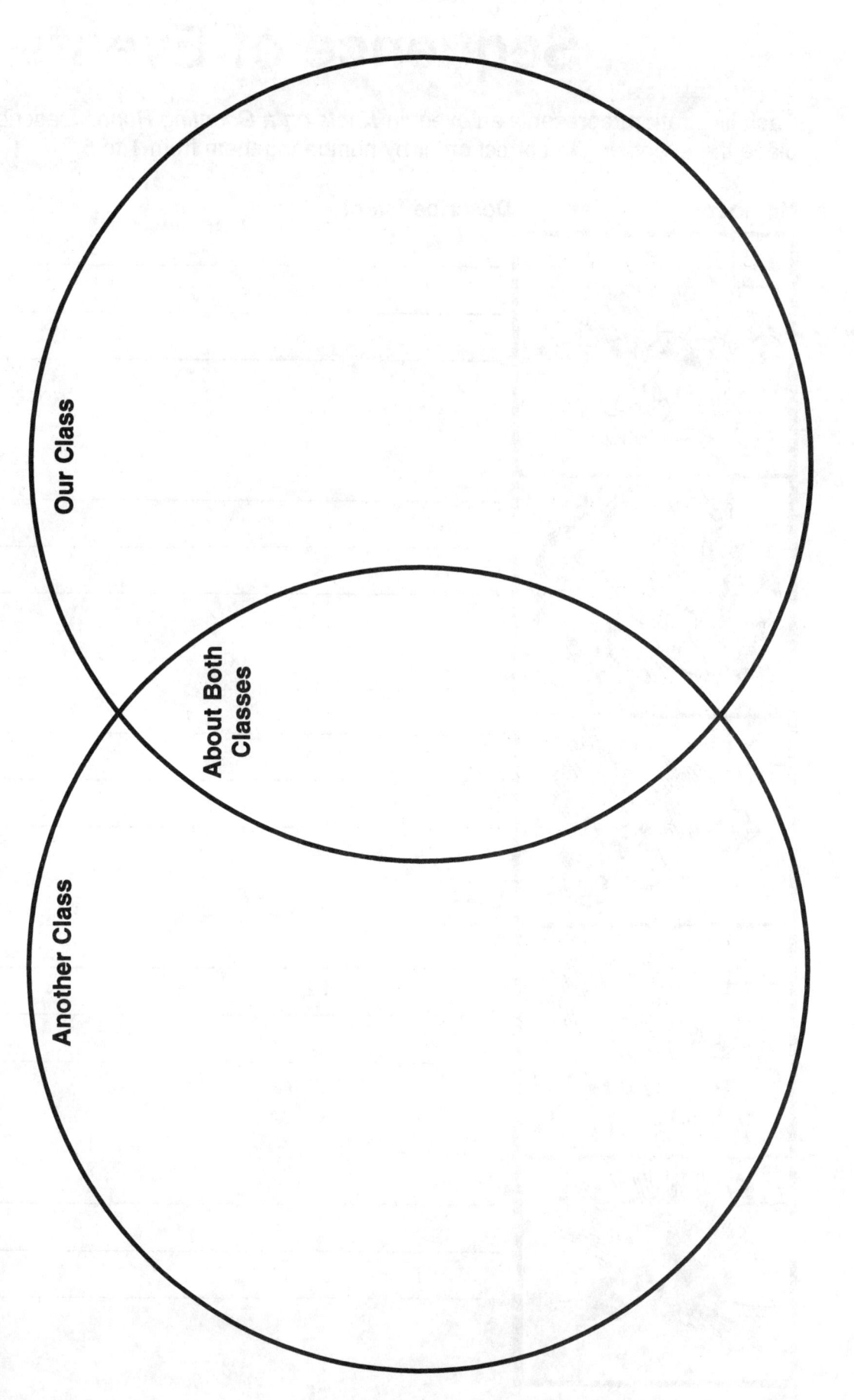

Our Class

About Both Classes

Another Class

© *Teacher Created Materials, Inc.* 99 #476 *Learning Through Literature—Native Americans*

Southwest

Name _____ Date _____

Sequence of Events

Each illustration represents an event in *Knots on a Counting Rope*. Describe each event and place the events in the correct order by numbering them from 1 to 5.

Number   **Describe Event**

_____
_____
_____
_____

_____
_____
_____
_____

_____
_____
_____
_____

_____
_____
_____
_____

_____
_____
_____
_____

#476 Learning Through Literature—Native Americans
© Teacher Created Materials, Inc.

Southwest

Name _____ Date _____

True or False

Read each sentence and decide whether it is true or false. Then circle the code letter that shows your answer.

_____ 1. Grandfather is kind.

_____ 2. The boy was named after his grandfather.

_____ 3. The boy couldn't see well.

_____ 4. There was a storm when the boy was born.

_____ 5. The boy liked horses.

_____ 6. Grandfather died.

_____ 7. The boy read stories to grandfather.

True	(A)	P	N	R	W	T	K
False	T	I	Q	U	M	O	B

Now write the circled letters in the blanks to find out something the boy loved. Draw a picture of what the boy loved.

___ _A_ ___ ___ ___ ___ ___
 4   1   2   3   7   6   5

© Teacher Created Materials, Inc.   101   #476 Learning Through Literature—Native Americans

Northwest

Brother Eagle, Sister Sky

Author: Susan Jeffers

Illustrator: Susan Jeffers

Publisher: Scholastic Inc., 1991

Summary: This book conveys an important message about our environment that was delivered more than a century ago by several of the great Native American Chiefs, including Chief Seattle.

Prereading Activity:

Show the students the cover of the book and then read the first page about Chief Seattle's meeting with the commissioner of Indian Affairs in Washington, D.C. Ask the students to predict what they think Chief Seattle will say. Read the story and then compare the students' predictions with what they read.

Key Words, Concepts, and People:

- ancestors
- slaughtered
- wilderness
- crests
- survival
- preserve
- prairie
- sap

Postreading Discussion Questions:

1. How do you think Chief Seattle would feel if he could see the world as it is today? *(Answers may vary.)*

2. How might the world be a different place to live if the Native Americans had not lost their land to the white settlers? *(Answers may vary.)*

3. Why did Chief Seattle agree to sell the Indians' land? *(He agreed because the white settlers won the wars.)*

4. What do you like best about the book? Least about the book? *(Answers may vary.)*

5. Describe Chief Seattle. Do you think you would like him? Why or why not? *(Answers may vary.)*

6. Is *Brother Eagle, Sister Sky* a good title for this book? Why or why not? *(Answers may vary.)*

Brother Eagle, Sister Sky (cont.)

Learning Activities:

- **America Then and Now (page 104)** Discuss how America has changed since the days when Chief Seattle lived. Display illustrations and discuss.

- As a class, write a different ending to *Brother Eagle, Sister Sky* in which the Native Americans do not lose their land to the white settlers.

- Have students write a class letter to be sent to the United States Bureau of Indian Affairs or an area office near you. Ask for such information as: How many Native Americans are there living in the United States today? Where do they live? What resources are available to learn more about Native Americans?

United States Department of the Interior
Bureau of Indian Affairs
1951 Constitution Avenue, NW
Washington, DC 20245
Area Offices

Aberdeen, SD	115 Fourth Ave., SE, 57401
Albuquerque, NM	PO Box 26567, 615 N. 1st St., 87125-6567
Anadarko, OK	PO Box 368, 73005
Billings, MT	316 N. 26th St., 59101
Juneau, AK	PO Box 3-8000, 99802
Minneapolis, MN	15 S. 5th St., 55402
Muskogee, OK	Old Federal Building, 77401
Phoenix, AZ	PO Box 7007, 3003 N. Central, 85011
Portland, OR	PO Box 3785, 1425 NE Irving St., 97208
Sacramento, CA	2800 Cottage Way, 95825

- Invite several Native Americans to your classroom to discuss how they reconcile living in two very divergent cultures. Ask them to discuss what it means to be bicultural. What are the advantages? What are the problems? In addition, ask them to share such things as the tribal histories, legends, foods, crafts, games, and dances of their people. Allow time for discussion and questions.

- **Acrostic Fun (page 105)** Introduce the concept of an acrostic—in which the letters of a word are used as the beginning to other words that relate to the first word. Assign the activity sheet. Allow time for students to share their own acrostics.

- **Word Cards (page 106)** and **Sentences (page 107)** Create a concentration game by photocopying, laminating, and cutting apart the boxes with words and sentences. Allow students to play the game by matching the word with the sentence it completes.

Northwest

Name_____ Date_____

America Then and Now

In the top box, draw a picture of the way America looked when Chief Seattle was alive. In the bottom box, draw a picture of the way America looks now.

#476 Learning Through Literature—Native Americans 104 © Teacher Created Materials, Inc.

Northwest

Name _____ Date _____

Acrostic Fun

Using the letters of Chief Seattle's name, write at least one word describing Chief Seattle that begins with each letter. This is called an acrostic. The first one is done for you.

<u>C</u>onsiderate

H _____   _____
I _____   _____
E _____   _____
F _____   _____
S _____   _____
E _____   _____
A _____   _____
T _____   _____
T _____   _____
L _____   _____
E _____   _____

Using the letters of your first and last names, create an acrostic describing yourself. Draw a picture of yourself.

© Teacher Created Materials, Inc.   105   #476 Learning Through Literature—Native Americans

Northwest

Word Cards

ancestors	crests
struggled	sap
slaughtered	prairies
preserve	wilderness

Northwest

Sentences

Chief Seattle told about the voices from his _____.

White settlers needlessly _____ the buffalo.

Native Americans _____ to keep their lands.

Native Americans once lived in the _____.

We crossed the Rocky Mountains _____.

Chief Seattle said the _____ in the trees is like blood in his veins.

Everyone should help to _____ the land, air, and rivers.

Most Native Americans are gone from the dusty _____.

© Teacher Created Materials, Inc. 107 #476 Learning Through Literature—Native Americans

North and Southeast

Little Firefly: An Algonquian Legend

Author: Terri Cohlene

Illustrator: Charles Reasoner

Publisher: Watermill Press, 1990

Summary: This book recounts the legend of a poor girl who seeks out a mighty, but invisible, hunter. It also describes the Algonquian, Native Americans of the Northeast.

Prereading Activities:

The Native Americans have always been great storytellers. Tell students that you will read a tale that the adult Algonquians used to tell their children. Show the title of the book and the picture on the cover and ask students to predict what the story might be about. Discuss with students the importance of storytelling in an era of no radio or TV. Elicit whether students have heard storytellers today.

Key Words, Concepts, and People:

- wigwam
- wampum
- Star Bridge of Souls
- Great Lakes
- Algonquian
- sinew

Postreading Discussion Questions:

1. Why was Little Firefly able to see the invisible warrior even though her sisters could not? *(According to the legend, Little Firefly was the one chosen to be his wife so she was given the power to see him.)*

2. Does this story remind you of a story you have heard many times before, perhaps a fairy tale? *(It is very similar to the story of Cinderella, in which a young girl who is mistreated by her older sisters wins the man—the Prince—that her sisters wanted. Even her nickname, Little Burnt One, is similar to the name Cinder-Ella.)*

3. The Algonquian were Native Americans who lived in the woodlands, or forests. What are some of the things they did to survive in the forests? *(They made wigwams, or houses, of wood; built canoes of birch bark so they could travel on the lakes; fished, farmed, and hunted for moose and other animals.)*

4. Who probably were the first European settlers that the Algonquian met? *(The Pilgrims were probably first.)*

5. Do you think Little Firefly's sisters treated her fairly? Why or why not? *(Answers may vary.)*

6. What did you like best about the story? *(Answers may vary.)*

North and Southeast

Little Firefly: An Algonquian Legend *(cont.)*

Learning Activities:

- Show students a map of the United States. Using the map on page 34 of the book, indicate the area that was once the home of the Algonquian Indian tribes. Have students identify the states in which the tribes lived. Tell students that the Algonquian people lived in wigwams that could hold as many as four or five families.

- Show the class the picture of the wigwam on page 39 of the book and have students draw a picture of a wigwam. Discuss that they were made of wood covered with animal skins and why there would be a hole in the top of the wigwam (so that smoke from the fire could escape).

- Algonquian women wore belted dresses or skirts of animal skin left open on the side. Children wore nothing in the summer, and in the winter they wore fur robes to protect themselves against the cold. Algonquian men were usually naked except for moccasins and a very small wrap around their waists. In the winter, they wore robes of animal skins. Find pictures of the Algonquian clothing from encyclopedias or books about Native American Indians and show them to the class.

- Discuss with students that buffalo were important to the Plains Indians, but that buffalo did not live in the Northeast. Have students brainstorm the kinds of animals that were hunted and trapped by the Algonquian people (muskrat, fox, rabbit, beaver, and moose).

- Tell students that to hunt deer, the Algonquian men often wore the skin and horns of a deer to trick the deer into thinking that the men were not humans so that the men could get closer and make it easier to kill the deer. Ask students to draw a picture of an Algonquian man dressed like a deer, preparing for the hunt.

- Tell students that the Iroquois, one part of the Algonquian tribe, had specific rules for men and women. Men hunted and waged war. Women controlled life within the village, grew crops, stored and managed the food, and supervised the harvest. Men owned only their clothing and weapons; women owned everything else. Discuss with the class how this compares with the roles men and women play in today's society.

- **Time to Eat (page 110)** Discuss with students the resources the Algonquian people had for growing, gathering, hunting, and preparing food, such as bone and stone knives, gourd pots, grinding stones, and open fires. Assign the activity sheet and have volunteers share their menus with the class.

- **The Three Sisters (page 111)** Discuss with the class reasons why Native Americans referred to corn, bean, and squash as "the three sisters." These reasons include that these three vegetables grew well in the same soil and plot and together they provided a healthful diet. Therefore, the Indians felt the vegetables must be related in a family sense. Assign the activity sheet and allow time for students to read aloud their stories.

- **Clans (page 112)** Discuss with students the concept of a clan. Also discuss why certain clans may choose certain animals to represent their clans. Assign the activity sheet. Have students read aloud their clan names and group students into "clans" according to the animals they chose. Then have each clan present their animal symbol to the class.

North and Southeast

Name _____ Date _____

Time to Eat

Consider the fruits, vegetables, and meat available to the Algonquian people and the resources they had to prepare them. Make a menu of meals they might have had.

Resources Available	
deer meat	berries
smoked fish	pumpkin seeds
trout	maple syrup
squash	lard
beans	corn

Breakfast
1. _____
2. _____
3. _____

Lunch
1. _____
2. _____
3. _____

Dinner
1. _____
2. _____
3. _____

How do these meals compare to what you eat? _____
_____

#476 Learning Through Literature—Native Americans   110   © Teacher Created Materials, Inc.

North and Southeast

Name _____ Date _____

The Three Sisters

Native Americans relied heavily on the important crops corn, beans, and squash. Write a legend about how these plants came to be called "The Three Sisters."

The Three Sisters

_____
_____
_____
_____
_____
_____
_____
_____
_____
_____
_____
_____
_____
_____
_____
_____

North and Southeast

Name _____ Date _____

Clans

Read about a certain clan and fill in the blanks.

The Bear Clan

An extended family, which means one composed of several families, was called a clan. Each clan identified an animal to honor. They chose this animal because of the characteristics they felt it possessed and that they wanted to have. The bear clan was a clan that was powerful and yet peaceful. Members of the bear clan did not eat bear meat. They placed the bear's head on top of a pole as a symbol of honor. They also used bearskin to decorate their wigwams.

My Clan

Name: _____

Animal Symbol: _____

Characteristics: _____

Favorite Foods: _____

How we honor and show respect to our animal:

_____
_____
_____
_____
_____
_____
_____
_____
_____

North and Southeast

Pocahontas, Daughter of a Chief

Author: Carol Greene

Publisher: Children's Press, 1988

Summary: This is a biography of the famous Indian woman, Pocahontas, who saved the life of Captain John Smith, the leader of the English colonists at Jamestown.

Prereading Activity:

Discuss with students the arrival of white people in what is now the eastern United States. Remind them of the Pilgrims and then tell them that other groups were arriving in different places along the coast. Lead a discussion about what the Native Americans might have thought about seeing these strange visitors come to their land from the sea and whether they would have been friendly or not.

Key Words, Concepts, and People:

- colonists
- war club
- armor
- attack
- Jamestown
- England

Postreading Discussion Questions:

1. What is the difference between a biography and fiction? *(A biography is the life story of real person while fictional characters are invented by the author.)*

2. Why do you think Pocahontas saved John Smith's life? *(Answers may vary but could include that she had made friends with him at the colony; she thought the Indians and the whites should live peaceably together.)*

3. Why did Pocahontas consider John Smith to be her brother? *(Among the many tribes, when someone saved someone else's life, that made them brothers.)*

4. Why did the English kidnap Pocahontas? *(The Indians were fighting the English, and the English wanted to hold her as a hostage to force her father, the Chief, to make peace.)*

5. Why did the English want Pocahontas to go to England? *(The settlers felt that in England, Pocahontas would make a good representative for the Indians of the New World and help people get to know them better. They believed that if people saw how friendly and peaceful she was, more colonists would want to go to America.)*

© Teacher Created Materials, Inc. 113 #476 Learning Through Literature—Native Americans

North and Southeast

Pocahontas, Daughter of a Chief (cont.)

Learning Activities:

- Tell students that Pocahontas is a biography of the daughter of an Indian chief. Ask them if they have read stories about other women. Discuss whether they were biographies or autobiographies (written by the person herself). Bring in some sample books for the class to review and read.
- Display a map of the United States. Identify Jamestown, Virginia, where the English settlers came and where Pocahontas first saw them. Ask them to identify the states surrounding Virginia.
- **Same and Different (page 115)** Discuss with students how the Indians differed from the European people who came to their lands. Then discuss how the people were the same. Assign the activity sheet. **Additional Answers:** Same—Both peoples worked very hard to get enough food: Different—The English had large ships while the Indians had only small canoes. The English had guns while the Indians only had bows and arrows.
- Divide the students into five groups. Have each group research one of the people or places important during the time Pocahontas lived. Have each group present a summary of their findings to the class. Research suggestions: Jamestown, John Smith, James Furr, Chief Powhatan, Captain Samuel Argall.
- **Important Dates in the Life of Pocahontas (page 116)** Assign the activity sheet.
  Answers: 1. 18 2. 11 3. 1608 4. 3 to 4 5. approximately 19 6. approximately 1 7. 21
- Find a book in the library that provides a more detailed explanation of Pocahontas and her life. Read selected chapters to the students to provide a more complete understanding of this fascinating young woman. Rent the video of the Disney movie and discuss with the class the differences presented by the book and the movie.
- Pochahontas was a young woman who had a great deal of courage. On several occasions she took great risks. Ask students to identify several times in her life in which she took great risks.
- Drums were an important part of the Native American culture. Ask students to obtain the following materials to make their own drums. A clean round cardboard tub, such as a five gallon ice-cream tub, a small metal wastebasket, or an empty oatmeal box. Cover the tub or box with paper and draw designs on it that represent the type of designs Native Americans would put on their drums. Be sure to color them in. Then, using either rawhide, thin leather strips, or heavy paper cover the center part of the drum and tie a string around it very tightly. Now use two sticks to beat your drum. You may wish to decorate your drumsticks or a wooden spoon.

North and Southeast

Name _____ Date _____

Same and Different

Identify ways in which the English settlers and Pocahontas were the same and different. One is done for you.

Same	**Different**
1. They both wanted to protect their own people.	1. The clothes of the English settlers were very different. They wore hats, vests, stockings, and shoes. In general, they wore many more clothes.
2. _____	2. _____
3. _____	3. _____
4. _____	4. _____
5. _____	5. _____
6. _____	6. _____

© Teacher Created Materials, Inc.   #476 Learning Through Literature—Native Americans

North and Southeast

Name_____ Date _____

Important Dates in the Life of Pocahontas

Read the list of dates for things that happened to Pocahontas and then answer the questions.

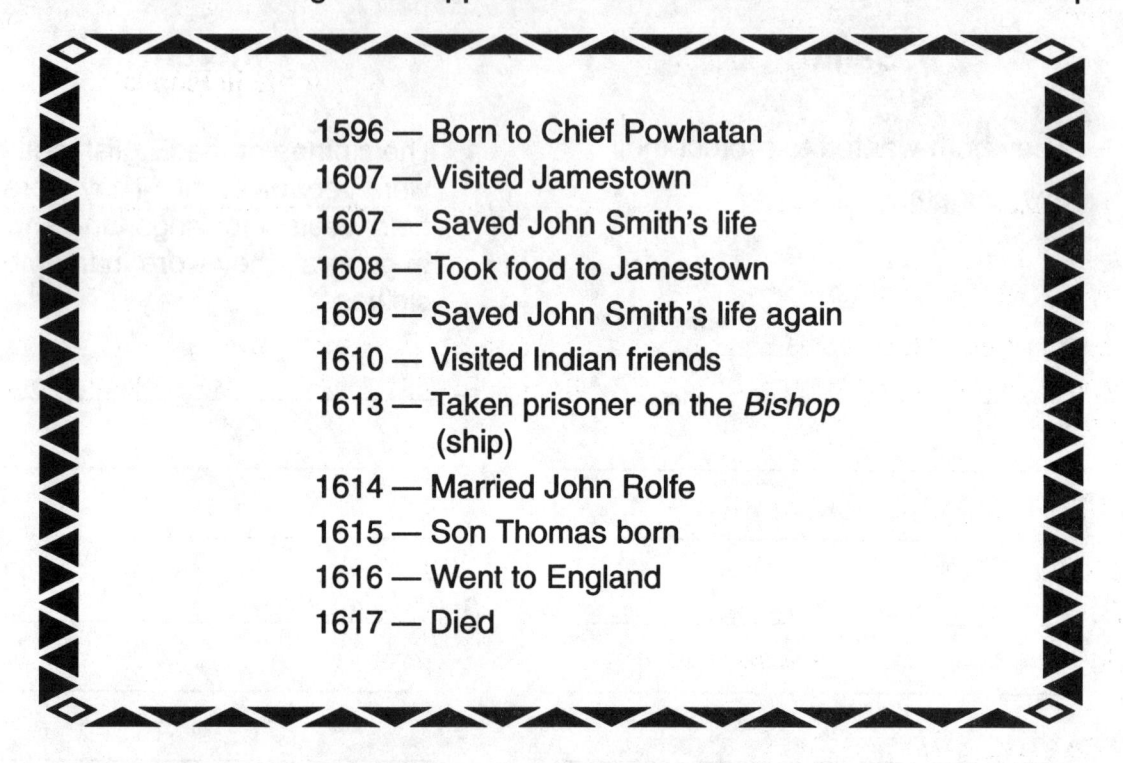

> 1596 — Born to Chief Powhatan
> 1607 — Visited Jamestown
> 1607 — Saved John Smith's life
> 1608 — Took food to Jamestown
> 1609 — Saved John Smith's life again
> 1610 — Visited Indian friends
> 1613 — Taken prisoner on the *Bishop* (ship)
> 1614 — Married John Rolfe
> 1615 — Son Thomas born
> 1616 — Went to England
> 1617 — Died

1. Approximately how old was Pocahontas when she married? _____

2. How old was Pocahontas when she first visited Jamestown? _____

3. During what year did she take food to Jamestown to help the people who were starving?
   _____

4. For how many years was she away, visiting her Indian friends? _____

5. What age was she when her son Thomas was born? _____

6. For how many years did she live in England? _____

7. How old was Pocahontas when she died? _____

   Use the dates about Pocahontas to make up your own question. Be sure to write the answer.

8. _____
   _____

#476 Learning Through Literature—Native Americans 116 © Teacher Created Materials, Inc.

North and Southeast

The Seminole

Author: Emilie U. Lepthian

Publisher: Children's Press, 1985

Summary: This book tells about the origin, history, and culture of the Seminoles and describes their life in Florida.

Prereading Activity:

Ask students if they have heard of the Seminoles, Native Americans who live in Florida in the Everglades. Discuss the environment of a swamp—What would people eat? What kind of homes would they build? What kind of clothing would they wear?

Key Words, Concepts, and People:

- chickee
- treaty
- Florida
- Creek
- Everglades
- tenant farmer
- hammock
- Osceola
- territory

Postreading Discussion Questions:

1. Who were the Seminole originally, and why did they move to Florida? *(They were part of a tribe called the Creek in southern Alabama and Georgia. The pressure of white settlers forced them into Florida.)*

2. Who frequently joined the Seminoles in Florida? *(Runaway slaves joined them.)*

3. What led to the first Seminole war? *(White settlers started moving into northern Florida, and the Seminole resisted. As a result, an American General, Andrew Jackson, invaded Florida and attacked the Seminoles.)*

4. Who was the most famous chief of the Seminole, and why? *(Osceola, "ah-see-oh-la" was the most famous. He refused to move when the government ordered all southeastern Native Americans to be moved west to what is now Oklahoma. Soldiers were sent to enforce the move, and the second Seminole war began. Osceola was tricked and captured. He died soon after that.)*

5. How did the Seminole live in the swamp? *(They found plots of high ground where they could build chickees, which are huts with raised platforms for floors and thatched roofs. They hunted, fished, and raised corn and other vegetables.)*

6. Are there still Seminoles in Florida? *(Yes, they live on reservations.)*

7. What kind of government do the Seminole have? *(They govern themselves with a democratic form of government.)*

North and Southeast

The Seminole (cont.)

Learning Activities:

- Have students reflect on the variety of Native American homes. Discuss with the class that the Seminoles built villages and huts, or chickees, on ground dry enough for farming. Chickees were on raised platforms that were open on the sides and in the front so that the air could circulate. The Seminoles slept in hammocks inside the chickees.

- **Dates Important in Seminole History (page 119)** Assign the activity sheet and answer the questions in class. **Answers:** 1. 10 years, 2. Spain, 3. 1819, 4. 1838, 5. 1835, 6. third Seminole war

- Explain to students that hunting was an important skill for males in Native American groups. Often boys took their bows and arrows first thing in the morning and practiced shooting moss or sticks that were thrown into the air by older men in the tribe. When a boy hit the stick or moss, he was then allowed to go and have breakfast. Ask students why they think it was so important for all of the males to be such good hunters.

- Ask for a volunteer to write to the Bureau of Indian Affairs, U.S. Department of the Interior, Washington, DC 20245 for more information about the Seminoles.

- **Go Fish (page 120)** Fishing was an important part of life for the Seminole. Assign the activity sheet, and ask student pairs to compare their "catches."

- Show the students a map of the United States. Ask them to locate southern Georgia and Alabama where the Seminole originated. Have them track the relocation of the Seminole to Florida and then to southeastern Oklahoma. Discuss these relocations in terms of whether they were voluntary or forced.

- **Seminole Language (page 121)** Hand out the activity sheet. Go over the pronunciations of the Seminole words with the class. Then have students complete the activity.

North and Southeast

Name_____ Date_____

Dates Important in Seminole History

Read what happened on the following dates and answer the questions below.

1790: Seminoles moved to Florida and established farms.
1812: United States troops did not go to Florida.
1817: General Andrew Jackson led troops into Florida and burned Seminole villages.
1819: United States bought Florida from Spain.
1822: Florida became a territory of the U.S.
1823: Seminoles sign a treaty with the U.S., allocating millions of acres of land.
1835: Second Seminole war began.
1842: Second Seminole war ended.
1837: Osceola agreed to talk to the American general.
1838: Osceola became ill and died.
1855: Third Seminole war began.
1858: Third Seminole war ended.
1905: Several tribes, including the Seminole, asked Congress to form an all Indian state in the southeastern part of Oklahoma.

1. For how many years did the second and third Seminole wars last altogether?
   _____
2. To what country did Florida belong until 1822? _____
3. In what year did the United States purchase Florida? _____
4. In what year did the great Seminole chief Osceola die? _____
5. In what year did the second Seminole war begin?_____
6. In 1855 the _____ began.
7. Make up your own question, using the important dates provided above.
   _____
   _____

© Teacher Created Materials, Inc.   119   #476 Learning Through Literature—Native Americans

North and Southeast

Name _____ Date _____

Go Fish

There are eight fish hiding in the water. Find the fish and color them.

North and Southeast

Name _____ Date _____

Seminole Language

Study the list of words. Then use Seminole words to complete the sentences below. Teach your family members some Seminole words.

---

children: *who-pish-co-cha*   little girl: *ta-goo-che*

brother: *cha-ta-che-kee*   father: *ta-tee*

my husband: *nu-nack-nee*   little boy: *nag-noo-che*

sister: *cha-foon-kee*   mother: *wa-a-chee*

my wife: *cha-hal-kee*

---

1. I am a _____.

2. Seminole call their children _____.

3. My mother is _____.

4. I call my brother _____.

5. _____ means "father."

6. A male can be _____, _____, _____, or _____.

7. To describe my sister I use _____.

8. Words that name a female are _____,
   _____, _____,
   and _____.

© Teacher Created Materials, Inc.   121   #476 Learning Through Literature—Native Americans

North and Southeast

The Chippewa

Author: Alice Osinski

Publisher: Children's Press, 1987

Summary: This book describes the woodland way of life of the Chippewa, Native Americans who lived around the Great Lakes in the northeastern part of the United States.

Prereading Activity:

Many Native Americans lived in woods and around lakes. Discuss with the class the ways people may have lived, dressed, eaten, and clothed themselves in woodland and lake areas.

Key Words, Concepts, and People:

- birchbark
- hunting grounds
- wigwam
- canoe
- game
- traps
- ceremony
- medicine woman
- snowshoes

Postreading Discussion Questions:

1. What did these woodlands Indians make their houses from? *(They made them from poles stuck in the ground and bent over and tied together. This frame was then covered with sheets of tree bark.)*

2. What are some of the things they made from the parts of trees? *(They made bowls, spoons, fishnet, mats, containers, homes, and canoes.)*

3. Why do you think the Chippewa were so happy when the sap of the maple trees started running? *(The sap provided them with sweets to eat, such as maple syrup. It also meant that the long, cold winter was over and warm weather was on the way.)*

4. What happened to the land where the Chippewa lived? *(Settlers from the United States kept moving onto it until finally, around 1880, the Chippewa were forced onto reservations.)*

5. Look at the pictures on page 39. The picture on the left shows three Native Americans in their native dress, and the picture on the right is the same three people in the modern clothes of the time. How are they different? *(Answers may vary.)*

North and Southeast

The Chippewa (cont.)

Learning Activities:

- Show students the map of the United States. Using the map on page 7 of the book, have students identify the names of the states in which the Chippewa once lived. Be sure to indicate to students that they lived in Canada and the United States.
- Explain to students that the Chippewas built their houses, called wigwams, using sticks and bark from trees. Take students on a walk in the area and have each one gather eight to ten sticks six to ten inches (15 cm to 25 cm) long and pick up an assortment of leaves and bark. Have students make their own wigwams by tying the sticks together at the top, spreading the bottoms into a circle, and gluing the leaves and bark on the outside of this frame.
- Remind students that the canoe was an important part of the Chippewa life. Ask students to make a list of all of the activities for which the Chippewa used the canoe. Next to each of the activities, indicate whether it was for transportation, food, or recreation.
- **Chippewa Food (page 124)** Assign the activity sheet for students to list the foods that the Chippewa ate. **Additional Answers:** corn, sturgeon, squirrels, nuts
- **Chippewa Life Then and Now (page 125)** Discuss with students that when the Chippewa owned their own land, the life they lived was very different from the life they live now that the government owns it. Assign the activity sheet and have volunteers tell how Chippewa life changed.
- **Lost in the Woods (page 126)** Assign the activity sheet in which students follow a maze.
- **Complete the Chippewa Story (page 127)** Assign the activity sheet, and call on students to each read aloud a sentence in the story.

North and Southeast

Name _____ Date _____

Chippewa Food

Several of the food sources used by the Chippewa are listed. Add at least five more foods. Then categorize the food as fish, animal, fruits or vegetables.

Food of the Chippewa

wild rice _____   _____

salmon _____   _____

raspberries _____   _____

_____   _____

fish	animals	fruits/vegetables
_____	_____	_____
_____	_____	_____
_____	_____	_____
_____	_____	_____
_____	_____	_____

From each of the categories, select one food that you would most like to eat and write them on the lines below. Tell why you would choose those foods.

_____
_____
_____
_____
_____

North and Southeast

Name _____ Date _____

Chippewa Life Then and Now

The life of the Chippewa Indian has changed considerably since the United States government took over their land and they were moved onto reservations. In each of the columns, write a sentence about how the Chippewa life has changed. The first one is done for you.

Then	Now
Education Chippewa children were taught in their homes by family members.	**Education** Chippewa children go to American schools.
Food	**Food**
Housing	**Housing**
Job Roles	**Job Roles**

© Teacher Created Materials, Inc.   125   #476 Learning Through Literature—Native Americans

North and Southeast

Name _____ Date _____

Lost in the Woods

Help the Chippewa Indian boy find his way his way back to his wigwam.

#476 Learning Through Literature—Native Americans   126   © Teacher Created Materials, Inc.

North and Southeast

Name_____ Date_____

Complete the Chippewa Story

Choose words from the box below to complete the story.

Once upon a time, there was a young Chippewa boy named Blue Fox. Blue Fox was very proud of his family members who had lived long before him. In fact, as he grew older, his parents often told him about the many accomplishments of his _____. They told him about how they used to make _____, a meshlike material they dropped into water to gather up fish they caught.

His forefathers were excellent fishermen and very good hunters. They used to sell their furs to _____ who carried them to cities far away. When they went hunting, they left the _____ and traveled for days to find the wild _____ in the woods and near the lakes. Sometimes they would have to travel as far north as a country we now call _____. In order to travel in the wintertime, they would have to strap woven frames called _____ over their footwear so they could walk over the deep snow. Blue Fox wanted his people to be proud of him. So he decided to help repair the _____, which had been damaged during a storm and let in too much cold air.

He went to the forest and found a special tree, an _____, whose wood is tough and straight. He peeled the _____ off of this tree, took it to his wigwam, and repaired the damage. His parents were very proud of him.

ancestors	wigwam	ash	bark
Canada	ceremony	fishnet	fur traders
game	died	village	hunting grounds
medicine man	rice lakes	snowshoes	trading posts

Note: Fold under before reproducing.

    Answers:

1. ancestors
2. fishnet
3. fur traders
4. village
5. game
6. Canada
7. snowshoes
8. wigwam
9. ash
10. bark

© Teacher Created Materials, Inc.　　127　　#476 Learning Through Literature—Native Americans

North and Southeast

The Mohawk

Author: Jill Duvall

Publisher: Children's Press, 1991

Summary: This book describes the history and the culture of the Mohawk, an Iroquois tribe of Native Americans in the northeastern United States.

Prereading Activity:

Discuss with the class where in the United States the Mowhawk Indians lived. If they focus only on the West, remind them of the story of the first Thanksgiving. The Mohawk lived in the same general area as where the Pilgrims first met Native Americans.

Key Words, Concepts, and People:

- sachem
- wampum
- clan
- longhouse
- warrior
- council
- totem
- alliance
- lacrosse

Postreading Discussion Questions:

1. What was the great agreement made by the tribes of the Iroquois? *(They agreed to replace the constant war between the tribes with peace. Sachems from all the tribes—Mohawk, Oneida, Seneca, Onondaga, and Cayuga—agreed to the Great Law of peace.)*

2. What was wampum and what role did it play in the Great Law? *(Wampum is strips of patterned beadwork. People used wampum to remember rules and agreements such as the Great Law. It was also used in many ceremonial ways during negotiations.)*

3. What was a clan among the Mohawk? *(The people of the tribe were divided up into clans. Each one was represented by a totem, usually a representation of an animal. Among the Mohawk, the clans were the Turtle, Bear, and Wolf. All the members of one clan were considered to be related, even across tribal boundaries.)*

4. How did the Mohawk get their food? *(They hunted and fished but also grew food crops, mainly corn, beans, and squash.)*

5. For whom did the Mohawks fight in the Revolutionary War? *(The Mohawks fought for the British, and when the British lost, they were run off their land by the victorious Americans. The British gave them land farther north near the St. Lawrence River.)*

6. What work do many of the Mohawks do today? *(Many are iron and steel workers who work high above the ground during the construction of new buildings.)*

7. What is one of the interests of one of their present-day chiefs, Chief Jake Swamp? *(One of his interests is saving the environment and planting trees to help save Mother Earth.)*

North and Southeast

The Mohawk *(cont.)*

Learning Activities:

- Show students a map of the United States and identify the land that was once the homeland of the Mohawks (Iroquois). Ask students to name the states and areas that comprise what was once Mohawk land.

- Masks were an important part of some of the Native American tribes, including the Mohawk. Show the class the picture of the mask on page 10. Have students draw masks and name them. Allow time for students to share their masks.

- **Wampum (page 130)** Assign the activity sheet in which students draw pictures of and describe wampum.

- **Mohawk Puzzle (page 131)** Assign the activity sheet and have pairs of students check their answers with each other. **Answers:** Across—1. tradition, 2. alliance, 3. longhouse, 4. sachem Down—1. tribe, 2. wampum, 3. warrior, 4. clan, 5. Iroquois, 6. totem

- Rent the movie *The Last of the Mohicans* and show excerpts to the class. Have students pay attention to the dress and the ways of the Indians. Discuss with them what they learned about the way the Mohicans interacted and the ways in which the Europeans acted.

- Tell students that the Mohawks developed many games that we still play today. Check out the book *Games of the North American Indians* by Stuart Culin (Dover Publications, 1975), and allow the class to play some of the games.

- Remind students that sachem was the word for chief. Tell them that when a chief died, the tribe felt it was like a tree being uprooted. They had to then decide who the new chief was, or plant a new tree. The new chief was formally introduced at the Great Council where all of the five nations met.

- Ask for volunteers to write a letter to the Museum of the Iroquois to obtain more information about this tribe. Address: Schoharie Museum of the Iroquois Indians, PO Box 158, Schoharie, NY 12157.

- Five tribes joined together: the Mohawk, Oneida, Seneca, Onondaga, and Cayuga. When these tribes united, the French referred to them as the Iroquois. The Indians referred to themselves as Haudenosaunee, which means "people of the longhouse." Brainstorm with students the advantages of the tribes becoming one.

North and Southeast

Name _____ Date _____

Wampum

Wampum was used to remember and record events that were important to the tribe. Wampum was made by arranging beads in special patterns. On the three belts below, draw a wampum design. Under each belt, tell what the design means.

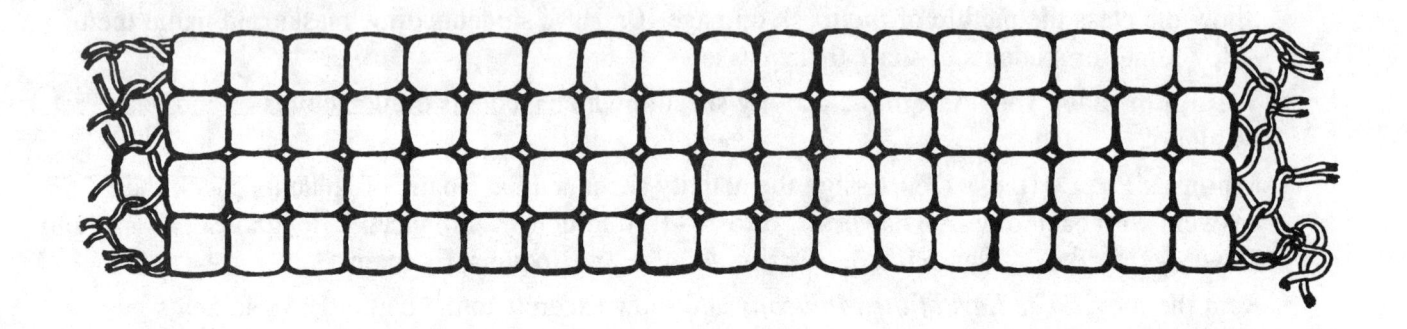

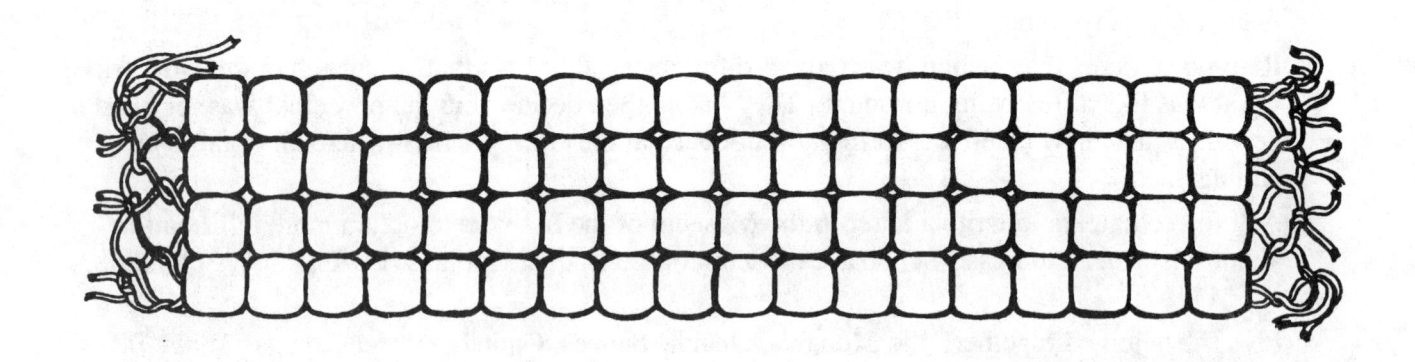

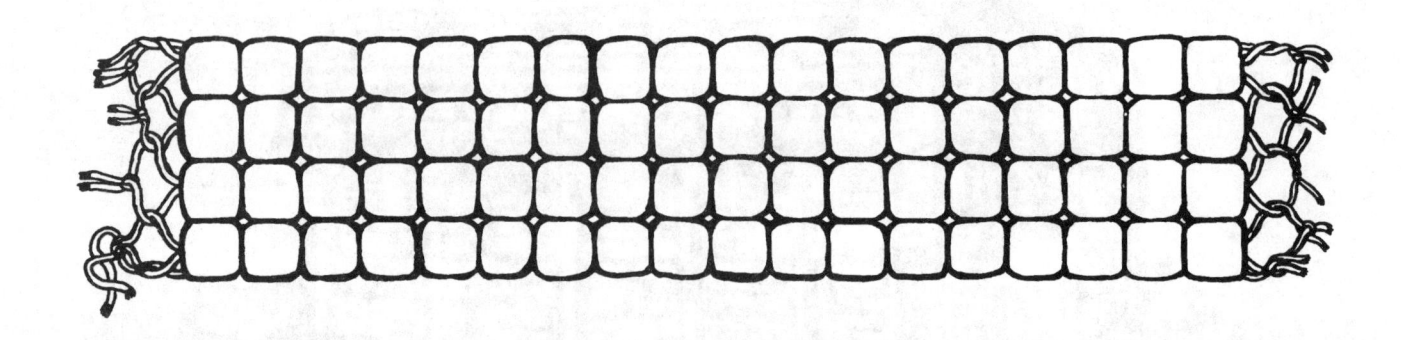

#476 Learning Through Literature—Native Americans © Teacher Created Materials, Inc.

Name _____ Date _____

North and Southeast

Mohawk Puzzle

Complete the crossword puzzle with important words about the Mohawks.

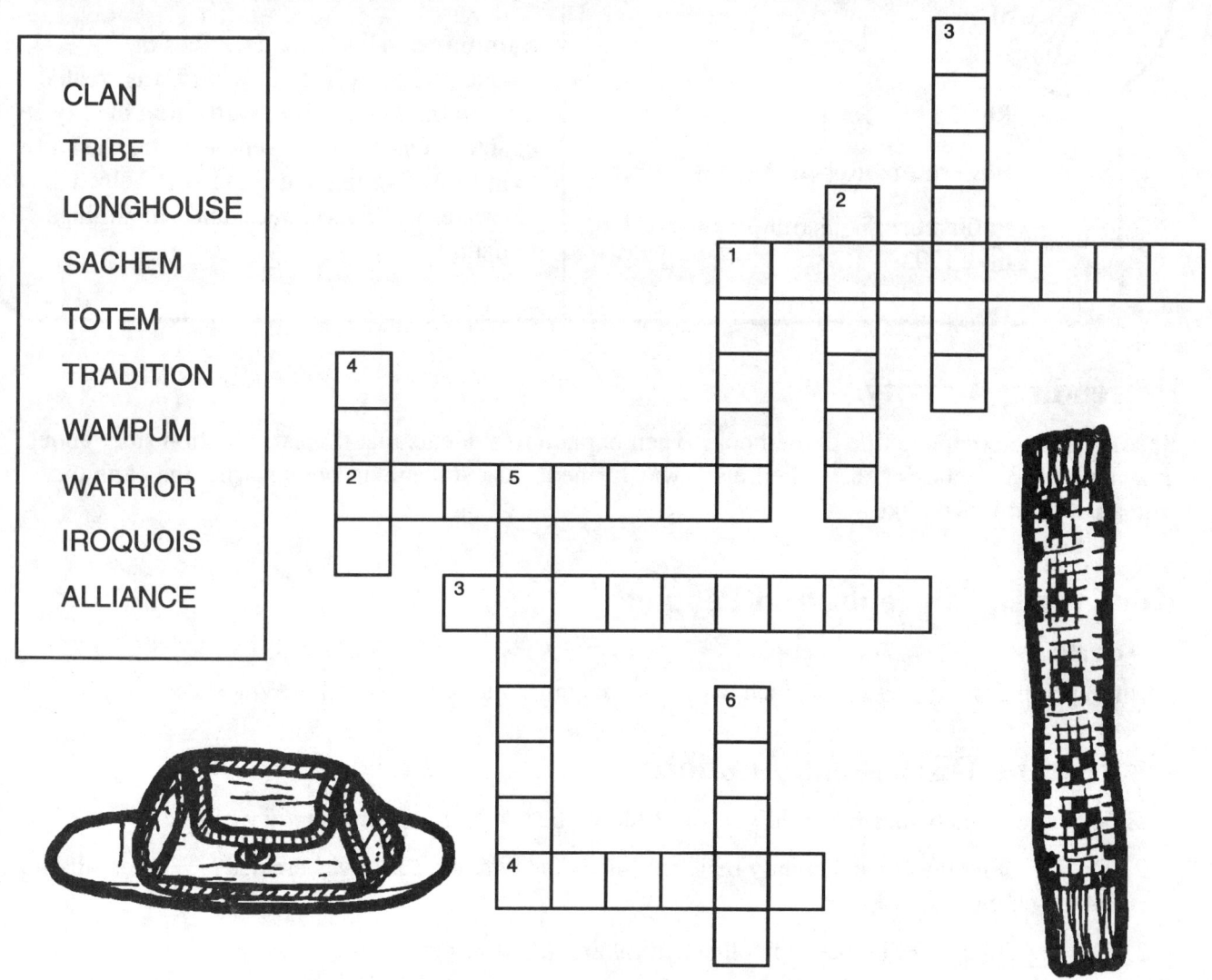

CLAN
TRIBE
LONGHOUSE
SACHEM
TOTEM
TRADITION
WAMPUM
WARRIOR
IROQUOIS
ALLIANCE

Across

1. way things have always been done
2. joining together
3. a long narrow building covered with sheets of bark
4. a chief in the Iroquois tribe

Down

1. people related by blood and customs
2. small beads used to record events and as money
3. a person in the tribe trained for fighting
4. related families, usually from a common ancestor
5. the French name for the tribe of five nations
6. an object that serves as a symbol for a clan

© Teacher Created Materials, Inc.　　　131　　　#476 Learning Through Literature—Native Americans

North and Southeast

The Woman Who fell From the Sky

Retold by: John Bierhorst

Illustrator: Robert Andrew Parker

Publisher: William Morrow and Co., Inc., 1993

Summary: This book describes the Iroquois view of how the world was created by a woman who fell to earth from the sky country. Once she arrived on earth, she had twin sons, Sapling and Flint, who helped her to create fish, rivers, trees, and other things in nature.

Prereading Activity:

Read aloud the complete title of the book. Then explain to students that this is a creation story about how the Iroquois nations believe their earth was formed. Ask students to predict what the earth the woman created looked like.

Key Words, Concepts, and People:

- creation
- footprints
- sky people
- sky woman
- ripples
- underground
- universe
- Milky Way

Postreading Discussion Questions:

1. Which of the characters would you most like to be? Why? *(Answers may vary.)*

2. Do you think the Iroquois really believed this is the way the earth was created? Why or why not? *(Answers may vary.)*

3. Did Sapling and Flint like each other? Explain. *(Answers may vary.)*

4. The Sky Woman, Flint, and Sapling created many things on the earth. What things can you think of that we have on earth today that they did not create? *(Answers may vary.)*

5. How do you think the Sky Woman felt about her husband and her sons? Explain. *(Answers may vary.)*

6. If you could change one thing about the earth that the Sky Woman and her sons created, what would it be? Why? *(Answers may vary.)*

The Woman Who fell From the Sky (cont.)

Learning Activities:

- Divide the story into four or five parts and assign the different parts to small groups of students to dramatize. Allow time for planning and rehearsing. Invite another class to be the audience.
- Have students draw pictures showing the creation of the earth according to this story.
- **Main Characters (page 134)** Discuss with the class the concept of main characters. Elicit from them the main characters in the story. Assign the activity sheet.
- **My Earth (page 135)** Assign the activity sheet in which students draw and describe a world they would create. Allow time to share their creations.
- **Compare and Contrast (page 136)** Discuss with the class how Sapling and Flint are alike and different they are from other members of their families. Assign the activity sheet.

Answers:

Same:

1. They were both boys; they both had the same mother; they both traveled along the Milky Way.

Different:

2. Sapling was gentle and Flint was hard as stone; Sapling was creative and giving and Flint was selfish and didn't think of others.

- As a class project, write a short story called "Our Class Story of Creation."
- **The Earth (page 137)** Assign this activity sheet on which students create an acrostic about things on earth.

North and Southeast

Name _____ Date _____

Main Characters

Read each phrase below and decide which character it best describes. Write the characters name next to the description. In the box, draw a picture of the character.

1. became jealous and uprooted the tree _____
2. threw a handful of earth into the sky and created stars _____
3. created monsters _____
4. made human beings _____
5. created fish _____
6. made falls and ripples in rivers _____

Sky Woman	Husband
Flint	Sapling

North and Southeast

Name _____ Date _____

My Earth

You have the power to create the earth. Draw a picture of what it will look like. Include land, animals, and vegetation you would put there.

© Teacher Created Materials, Inc. 135 #476 Learning Through Literature—Native Americans

North and Southeast

Name _____ Date _____

Compare and Contrast

Read and answer the following questions.

In what ways are Sapling and Flint alike?

_____
_____
_____
_____
_____
_____

In what ways are Sapling and Flint different?

_____
_____
_____
_____
_____
_____

Which character are you most like, Sapling or Flint? Explain.

_____
_____
_____
_____
_____
_____

North and Southeast

Name _____ Date _____

The Earth

On the lines beside the letters below, list as many things as possible that are found on the earth that begin with that letter.

C _____

R _____

E _____

A _____

T _____

I _____

O _____

N _____

Which do you wish were not on earth?
_____
_____
_____
_____

Why?
_____
_____
_____
_____
_____
_____

© Teacher Created Materials, Inc. 137 #476 Learning Through Literature—Native Americans

North and Southeast

Corn Is Maize: The Gift of the Indians

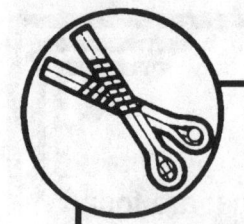

Author: Aliki

Publisher: Thomas Y. Crowell Co., 1976

Summary: This book tells the history of corn—how it was cultivated through the years, how the Indians shared their knowledge with the Pilgrims, and about many of the good things that come from corn.

Prereading Activity:

Corn Is Maize: The Gift of the Indians is a story about how the corn plant was discovered and the many good things that come from this plant. Discuss with students what good things they know about that come from the corn plant. List them on the chalkboard. Tell students to keep in mind what they know about corn and what they learn as they read.

Key Words, Concepts, and People:

- maize
- corn silk
- pollen
- tassel
- Indian
- tribes
- kernel
- husks

Postreading Discussion Questions:

1. How do the tiny grains of pollen get from the tassels to the silk of the corn plant? *(Summer breezes blow them.)*

2. What other plants belong to the same grain family as corn? *(Wheat, rye, oats, barley, and rice are in the corn family.)*

3. What are some of the different ways Indians used corn as food? *(They ate corn on the cob, popcorn, tortillas, tacos, tamales, cornstalk "candy," dry cornmeal, corn bread, and mush.)*

4. What are some ways we use corn today? *(Answers may vary but could include corn oil, corn syrup, cereal, medicine, alcohol, soap, glue, and baby powder.)*

5. Many tribes depended on corn as their main food source. How did they show their appreciation for the corn? *(They prayed to Corn Gods and had festivals with music, dancing, and chanting.)*

6. How do you think the Indians felt about sharing their corn with the Pilgrims? Explain. *(Answers may vary.)*

7. Do you think corn is as important to people today as it was in the days of the Indians and Pilgrims? Explain. *(Answers may vary.)*

North and Southeast

Corn Is Maize: The Gift of the Indians (cont.)

Learning Activities:

- **Word Match (page 140)** To review words from the story, assign the activity sheet and go over the answers in class. **Answers:** maize, 3; Indian, 8; corn silk, 2; kernel, 5; tribe, 1; pollen, 7; husks, 4; tassel, 6.

- **Hidden Words (page 141)** Assign the activity sheet in which students do a word search.

- Bring in a bag of cornmeal and discuss that this is corn that is finely ground. Send a letter home with students, asking for a copy of one recipe in which corn or a corn product is used. Compile these into a class recipe book entitled "Our Corn Recipe Book." Make a copy for each student and ask for volunteers to make one of the recipes and bring it to class to share at a corn party.

Corn Bread

1 cup (250 mL) flour
³/₄ cup (188 mL) cornmeal
3 tbs. (45 mL) sugar
1 tbs. (15 mL) baking powder
¹/₂ tsp. (2.5 mL) salt
1 egg
¹/₃ cup (85 mL) melted butter or margarine
²/₃ cup (170 mL) milk

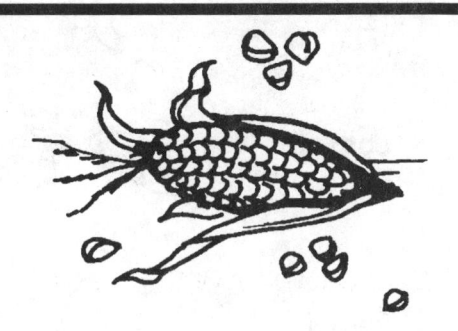

Preheat the oven to 425° F (220° C). Grease an 8" x 8" (20 cm x 20 cm) baking pan. With a fork, mix flour, cornmeal, sugar, baking powder, and salt together in a bowl. In another bowl, beat together the remaining ingredients. Pour mixtures together and stir just until the flour is moistened. Pour into greased pan and bake 25 minutes.

- **Growth Sequence (page 142)** Assign the activity sheet on which students will arrange pictures of the stages of corn growth in a grid. Sequence: Across—Top Row: 4, 7, 3; Middle Row: 2, 1, 8; Bottom Row: 6, 5, 9.

- **Cornhusk Doll (page 143)** Use 143 to let students have the opportunity to create a picture of a cornhusk doll.

- Entitle a bulletin board "Corn Is Maize." Have students cut out pictures in magazines or make drawings to show the different ways in which corn can be used. Display their pictures on the bulletin board.

- On the last page of the book are directions for making a cornhusk wreath. Provide wire clothes hangers, fresh cornhusks, and string, and have each student make a wreath.

- Obtain a copy of the book *Corn, What It Is, What It Does* by Cynthia Kellog (New York: Greenwillow, 1989). Read it aloud to the class and discuss it. Challenge students to think of different ways corn is used different from those they have already learned.

- **Dear Indians (page 144)** Discuss with the class the many things the Indians did to help the Pilgrims get started in their new land. Assign the activity sheet.

North and Southeast

Name _____ Date _____

Word Match

Match the meanings with the vocabulary words by putting the correct number in the blank in front of each word. The pictures will help you to make the matches.

_____ maize

_____ Indian

_____ corn silk

_____ kernel

_____ tribe

_____ pollen

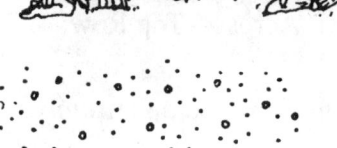

_____ husks

_____ tassel

1. a group of people who share a common ancestry

2. the female part of the plant that looks like thin threads and hangs out of the corn

3. another name for corn

4. a bundle of leaves that is wrapped tightly around the corn silk

5. a grain or seed

6. the male flower that grows like a hat at the top of the stalk

7. the powderlike material that fertilizes corn

8. the name Christopher Columbus gave to the people living in the New World

#476 Learning Through Literature—Native Americans　　140　　© Teacher Created Materials, Inc.

North and Southeast

Name _____ Date _____

Hidden Words

Find and circle the words hidden in the ear of corn below.

| pollen | grain | Indian | harvest |
| maize | wheat | husk | Pilgrim |

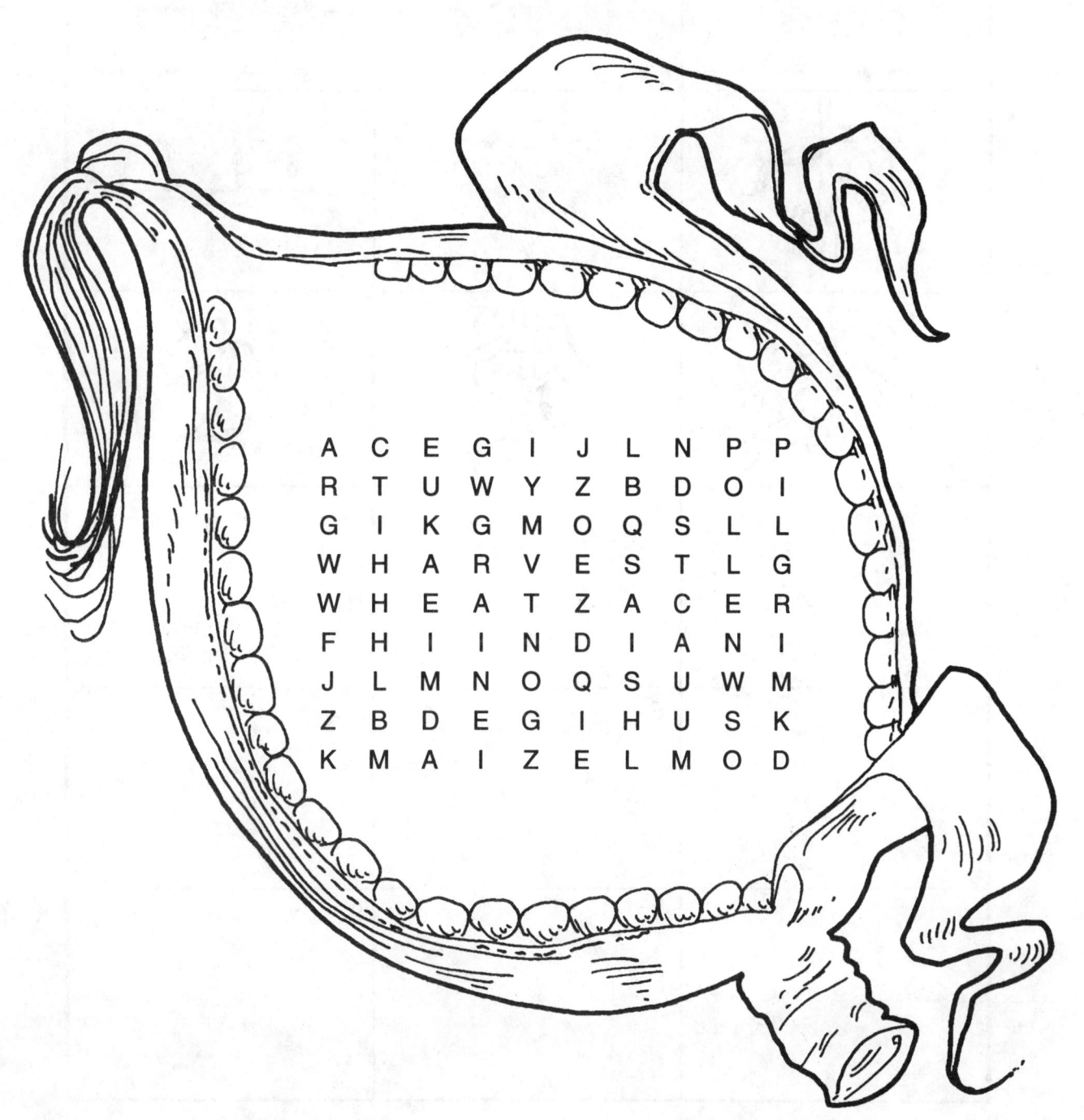

```
A C E G I J L N P P
R T U W Y Z B D O I
G I K G M O Q S L L
W H A R V E S T L G
W H E A T Z A C E R
F H I I N D I A N I
J L M N O Q S U W M
Z B D E G I H U S K
K M A I Z E L M O D
```

© Teacher Created Materials, Inc.   141   #476 Learning Through Literature—Native Americans

North and Southeast

Name _____ Date _____

Growth Sequence

Cut out the pictures below and in the boxes provided place them in the correct order for growing a plant.

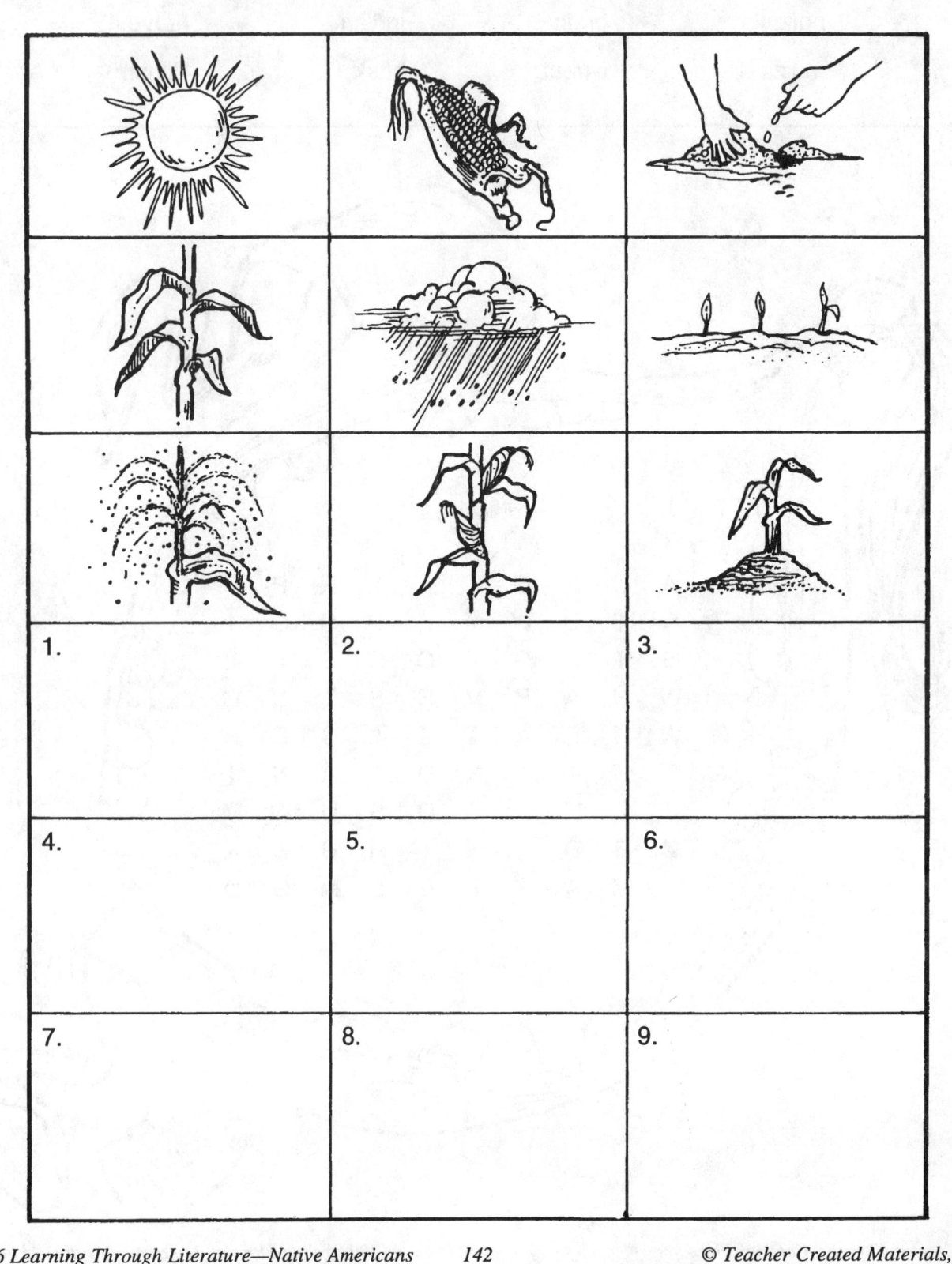

1.	2.	3.
4.	5.	6.
7.	8.	9.

#476 Learning Through Literature—Native Americans   142   © Teacher Created Materials, Inc.

North and Southeast

Name _____ Date _____

Cornhusk Doll

Draw a picture of a cornhusk doll. Tell how it is alike and how it is different from dolls of today.

Alike

_____
_____
_____
_____
_____
_____
_____

Different

_____
_____
_____
_____
_____
_____
_____

© Teacher Created Materials, Inc. 143 #476 Learning Through Literature—Native Americans

North and Southeast

Name _____ Date _____

Dear Indians

When the Pilgrims landed in America, the Indians saved their lives and taught them how to survive. Pretend you are one of the Pilgrims. Write the Indians a letter to thank them for all they did to help you get started in this new land. Use specific details.

_____
(*Date*)

Dear Indians, (*Greeting*)

_____
_____
_____
_____
_____
_____
_____
_____
_____
_____
_____
_____

(*Body*)

Your friend, (*Closing*)

_____
(*Signature*)

#476 Learning Through Literature—Native Americans   144   © *Teacher Created Materials, Inc.*